ADVANCE PRAISE FOR *THE INTR~~OVERT'S E~~DGE*

"This book will be a game changer for any introvert who hates selling or believes they just can't do it. You can!"
— Neil Patel, *New York Times* bestselling author of *Hustle* and co-founder of Crazy Egg & Hello Bar

"Here are all the fundamental techniques you need to become a successful salesperson! If you've ever felt that your introversion is an obstacle to your success, worry no more. Matthew Pollard shows you exactly why the opposite is true! For all of you introverts who are looking to succeed in sales (or any extrovert-dominated field), *The Introvert's Edge* by Matthew Pollard is for you!"
— Marshall Goldsmith, international bestselling author of *What Got You Here Won't Get You There*

"Matthew has created the ultimate guide for people who are reluctant to enter the world of sales. He won the war with his instinct, courage, friendliness, and honesty. But the cool part is he documented it so that you can do the same thing. More than a sales book, it's both informational and inspirational."
— Jeffrey Gitomer, author of *The Little Red Book of Selling*

"Don't read this book . . . if you love excuses. I used to believe that I couldn't sell because 'I'm an introvert.' This book taught me that my excuse was actually an advantage."
— Ryan Deiss, CEO, DigitalMarketer.com

"Introverts have what it takes to be great salespeople! Matthew Pollard proves that point and more in this compelling read. By sharing powerful case examples and a clear sales system, he offers introverts a way to build on their listening and preparation skills to win sales and influence people."
— Jennifer Kahnweiler, Ph.D., CSP, bestselling author of *The Introverted Leader* and *Quiet Influence*

"At the core, I'm an introvert myself, so I know the importance of reliable, adaptable systems that draw on our greatest strengths. Matthew Pollard has nailed a process that harnesses our creativity, empathy, and analytical thinking to cultivate relationships that create the solutions your customers need."

—Dr. Ivan Misner, founder of BNI and *New York Times* bestselling author of *Truth or Delusion? Busting Networking's Biggest Myths*

"I've long advocated taking control of the sale, while at the same time keeping the customer's needs front and center. Matthew Pollard's system does exactly that—and much more. Brilliant, intuitive, and refreshing."

—Matthew Dixon, author of *The Challenger Sale* and *The Challenger Customer* (listed as the number one and two Most Highly-Rated Sales Books of All Time by HubSpot)

"Sales is due for a transformation. *The Introvert's Edge* flips selling from an uncomfortable, unsuccessful, high-pressure nightmare to a smooth, winning conversation."

—Mark Roberge, Senior Lecturer at Harvard Business School; former CRO at HubSpot; bestselling author of *The Sales Acceleration Formula*

"Introverts can set the world on FIRE, and Matthew Pollard will show you how in *The Introvert's Edge*. Introverts, it's time to IGNITE!"

—John Lee Dumas, founder and host of *Entrepreneurs On Fire* (recently ranked by *Entrepreneur* as a top five podcast for entrepreneurs)

"Being an extrovert, this book by Matthew helps me understand why some of my biggest competitors in my sales career have been the quiet ones."

—Erik Day, Vice President & GM, North America Small Business at Dell Technologies

"Finally! A sales manual for people who'd rather chew their arm off than 'work a room' . . . in other words, most of us. I make much of my living trying to be an extrovert on stage by giving speeches. When I have to do what amounts to selling, I don't have any energy left. I need a sales system that doesn't rely on any natural ability for charm, chit-chat, or schmoozing. *The Introvert's Edge* is it."

—Paul Smith, bestselling author of *Sell with a Story*

"Everyone knows that introverts can't sell very well. Wrong! *The Introvert's Edge* provides the necessary steps to sell successfully, and it does so in an easy, accessible, and readable manner. Through the use of stories, this book goes way beyond general sales tips; it provides insights on how introverts can make the leap into sales. Ease into this book and you will see immediate results."

—John B. Molidor, Ph.D., President of the National Speakers Association and Professor of Psychiatry at Michigan State University

"*The Introvert's Edge* is a great read for both the quiet and the less-quiet. Matthew Pollard not only shows the power of process over personality when it comes to sales, but helps pave the way for workplaces that are great for all kinds of people."

—Ed Frauenheim, Director of Research and Content, Great Place to Work Institute

"Matthew Pollard really knows what he's talking about. Every introvert interested in selling any idea or product would be well advised to read his book and follow his simple and practical process."

—Derek Lidow, Professor of Entrepreneurship at Princeton and author of *Startup Leadership* and *Building on Bedrock*

"As a Sales Strategist instructor for our (then) young company, Matthew added hundreds of thousands of dollars in sales for us with his 'just tell stories' technique. He transformed our lowest selling introverted salesperson into a 'Top Dog' winner for highest quarterly sales. Now, he has distilled that several-week course into an enjoyable read that has you pulling for the introvert, all while absorbing Matthew's tried-and-true successful sales strategies. I highly recommend this book for both introverts and extroverts alike to improve their sales productivity."

—Volney Campbell, Co-Chairman/Principal at Colliers International Austin

"Matthew Pollard challenges some time-honored beliefs on what it takes to be successful at sales. I love how he weaves real-life stories into practical applications that new or even experienced reps can put to use right away! It's a must-read for anyone who proudly calls sales their profession!"

—Bob Perkins, founder and Chairman of the American Association of Inside Sales Professionals

"Matthew Pollard gets people, and he gets sales. *The Introvert's Edge* not only dispels the myth that you must be loud and outgoing to thrive in sales, but also offers a powerful roadmap for how all of us can better build trust and connect with buyers. I. Absolutely. Love. This. Book. I highly recommend it for anyone who sells, not just for those who are more reserved!"

—Mike Weinberg, author of the AMACOM bestsellers *Sales Management. Simplified.* and *New Sales. Simplified.*

"Disclaimer: I went into Matthew's book a skeptic. (Introverts make the best salespeople? C'mon.) By page 6, I was intrigued; by page 16, I was captivated—by page 30, Mr. Pollard had won another believer and raving fan. *The Introvert's Edge* isn't vague coaching, it isn't a rah-rah pep talk, it isn't a handful of interesting ideas. This is the real deal. Matthew's approach is gold. Not only sales gold, but gold, period."

—John David Mann, coauthor of *New York Times* bestseller *The Red Circle* and the bestselling classic *The Go-Giver*

"The more we learn about introversion, the better equipped we are to draw on its strengths. *The Introvert's Edge*, a fine addition to the canon of introvert advice, offers a concrete, clearly delineated plan to help introverts defy the misperception that they can't succeed in sales."

—Sophia Dembling, author of *The Introvert's Way* and *Introverts in Love*

"Matthew practices what he preaches: by naming our pain points and sharing inspiring success stories, he sells us on the idea that introverts can sell! His framework puts process over personality, which is music to this introverted entrepreneur's ears. I love how clearly he outlines his proven method. Whether you pick-and-choose or adopt his entire system, get ready to experience greater ease and flow with your sales process!"

—Beth L. Buelow, PCC, author of *The Introvert Entrepreneur* and host of *The Introvert Entrepreneur* podcast

"By far, this is the best sales book I have ever read. Matthew teaches how to turn every sales call from a pushy, do-or-die bulldog approach into a performance . . . much like a play. Tremendously effective for us introverts and a must-read for anyone who knows they need to learn to sell, but thinks they don't have what it takes."

—Brian Smith, UGG founder and author of *The Birth of a Brand*

"This book not only proves that introverts can be great at sales, it gives you the step-by-step tools to actually be great at sales."

—Jason Cohen, founder and CTO of WP Engine

"This wonderful book shows you how to sell in a warm, self-confident way, straight from the heart, by focusing on helping your customer make the best decision for him or her, with no pressure, which sows the seeds for a long-term relationship."

—Brian Tracy, motivational public speaker and author of *The Psychology of Selling*

"I love it when someone looks at sales differently! In *The Introvert's Edge*, Matthew Pollard provides a whole new take on sales and authentic selling. Matthew has managed to evolve tried and proven strategies into a system that offers predictable results. Unbelievable!"

—Tom Hopkins, author of *How to Master the Art of Selling* and *When Buyers Say No*

"Anyone thinking that sales isn't for them 'because they're an introvert' should read this book. For too long, introverts have believed that their personalities make them ineffective salespeople, or that they have some excuse not to learn and master the necessary skills. This book provides an overwhelming amount of evidence to the contrary. Sales is just a process, like anything else, that can be learned and perfected—and introverts are, in fact, uniquely suited to succeed in sales."

—Jordan Harbinger, co-founder and host of *The Art of Charm* podcast (ranked by *Forbes* as one of the 50 best relationship-builders in the world)

"Through simple advice and countless memorable stories, Matthew makes it clear that anyone can be successful in sales—even those who are introverted and shy. Open this book to discover how to create a sales system that will work for your business, that will grow with you, and most important, that will be authentically yours."

—Tony Vlahos, Chief Marketing Officer, ExecuNet

"I've been a professional speaker and author for over 40 years and was inducted into the Sales & Marketing Hall of Fame, yet I turn to my young mentor Matthew Pollard to help me continue to succeed. This amazing man has discovered a game-changing approach to common business challenges. Let him guide you through real world examples that you can relate to and learn from. Read this book now...and make your success easier tomorrow."

—Jim Cathcart, founder of Cathcart.com and author of *The Self Motivation Handbook, Relationship Selling,* and *The Acorn Principle*

"For too long, sales books have focused on bulldog sales techniques. Matthew provides a simple, relaxed, step-by-step system for people who don't want to sell...but need to stay in business."

—Julie Fedele, General Manager at Bupa Australia and New Zealand

"Matthew makes it clear that being an introvert is no excuse—it's an edge! Introverts, rejoice! This book offers a clear, practical, and proven system that will boost your confidence to close more deals than you ever thought possible."

—Gerhard Gschwandtner, founder and Publisher of *Selling Power* magazine

"A salesperson or small business owner achieves success in sales when they listen, hear, build trust, and advocate on behalf of their customer. This book does a masterful job of outlining all the key elements an introvert must use to obtain a successful sales outcome and, more important, a happy customer."

—Resa Kierstein, Vice President of Development at SCORE

"One of the best books on sales process and technique that I've ever read. Introverts empowered by this sales process will generate amazing results, regardless of their industry, title, or product. Every business owner and sales team should read this book."

—Justin McCullough, Vice President of National Small Business E-Commerce at Capital One

"Matthew's unique perspective on sales, and how introverts can master the process, has been sorely needed for a long time. A welcome addition to sales training literature, with ground-breaking advice and strategies. For too long, introverts have lived with the stigma that they can't succeed in this loud world of extroverts. It's a nice surprise to see someone confront this myth with not just research, but real-world evidence and application."

—Marco Rasi, founder and Executive Manager of Il Commerciale - The Salesman © and founder of the Best Sales Blogger Awards

"Relevant, relatable, and right-on-target insights and advice from an undisputed industry leader. A treasure trove of practical tips, relatable stories, and first-hand learnings that will revolutionize your approach to sales and literally transform your business."
—Brig. General (R) John E. Michel, C-Suite Leader, TED speaker, bestselling author, and internationally recognized expert in Positive Organizational Performance

"If you are an introverted business owner, you need this book. Sales are the lifeblood of your business and you can still be hugely successful even if you are an introvert—if you read this!"
—Jaime Masters, founder and host of the *Eventual Millionaire* (recently ranked by *Inc.* as a top three podcast for entrepreneurs)

"Matthew dissects the struggles that introverts like me have with sales, and he shows how we can excel in a realm thought to be the sole domain of the extroverted. I am already putting the lessons to good use in my job and will keep the book as a handy reference. Good reading and happy selling."
—Scott Healy, Partner Manager at Oracle

"The hard sell doesn't work in the new economy. Listening, peeling back the onion on the deep pain points that need to be solved, and knowing how to drive improvement are the new in-demand sales skills, and introverts master these instinctively. Matthew Pollard teaches you a repeatable process that really works."
—Rob Stone, National Partner Director, Xero Australia

"For too long, introverts have been at a disadvantage in the business world. But not anymore! *The Introvert's Edge* shows you how to harness your innate talents to succeed in sales, taking your career to the next level."
—Dorie Clark, author of *Stand Out* and *Entrepreneurial You*, and Adjunct Professor at Duke University's Fuqua School of Business

"Most freelancers like me choose to go out on our own so we can do what we love, on our own terms. We never really think about sales . . . until we don't have any. It's vital that we learn what Matthew's system provides—a clear, comfortable process that's actually not like selling at all."
—Emily Leach, founder of the Freelance Conference (recognized by *USA Today* as the #1 conference for freelancers to check out in 2017)

"The secrets are in this book. Matthew Pollard takes the guesswork and uncertainty out of sales, and turns it into a structured process that achieves results. If you're an introvert and think that sales is hard, think again. Matthew shows you it's more than just turning on the charm and bulldozing your way to the close. This is an insightful must-read for anyone who's into selling or wants to sell."

—Frazer Neo Macken, Vice President of Communications,
Electrolux Asia Pacific

"The book is fantastic and offers practical steps to support introverts in becoming better salespeople. A must-read for everyone wanting to become better at sales."

—Nick Hilton, head of Strategic Growth and Alliances
at NAB / MLC Advice Partnerships

"I encourage my students to learn from others' experiences and then adapt them for their own use. Matthew Pollard's *The Introvert's Edge* delivers these experiences brilliantly and offers a sales process that introverts—or anyone—could adapt and use right away. Pollard shows introverts that they, too, can be stellar salespeople. Highly recommended for both business students and business leaders who want to level up their sales skills."

—Harlan Beverly, Ph.D., Lecturer at McCombs School of Business
and Asst. Director of Texas Venture Labs, UT Austin

"The most comprehensive book on sales I've ever read, all wrapped up in fun stories that had me entertained the whole time. Whether you love or hate sales, *The Introvert's Edge* is for you. I am going to make sure my entire team reads it!"

—Jeff Yapp, founder and CEO of WUTZNXT and
former president of 20th Century Fox

MATTHEW POLLARD

WITH DEREK LEWIS

THE
introvert's
EDGE

How the Quiet and Shy
Can Outsell Anyone

HarperCollins
Leadership

An Imprint of HarperCollins

The Introvert's Edge

Published by HarperCollins Leadership, an imprint of HarperCollins Focus LLC.

Any internet addresses, phone numbers, or company or product information printed in this book are offered as a resource and are not intended in any way to be or to imply an endorsement by HarperCollins Leadership, nor does HarperCollins Leadership vouch for the existence, content, or services of these sites, phone numbers, companies, or products beyond the life of this book.

ISBN 978-0-8144-3887-9 (TP)

Printed in the United States of America

CONTENTS

CONTENTS

FOREWORD

I hate networking—it's icky and manipulative.

This is ironic, as I'm ranked as one of the top networkers in the world by *Forbes*, *Fast Company*, and *Bloomberg*, among others. But I don't think of what I do as networking. I see myself as a "connector." I love introducing two people who need to know each other. As soon as I meet someone, I begin thinking about how what they do could help someone I know. To me, I'm just connecting two people in an intentional way that serves their strategic purposes.

I get a special thrill at meeting unwitting geniuses. For some reason, incredibly skilled people—technicians, creatives, inventors, thinkers—are the last to recognize their talent. I enjoy helping these people craft investment pitches, nurturing them through the process, seeing them access exactly what they need, and watching the success that comes from them discovering their own magic. I love helping people promote themselves.

Again, it's ironic, because I hate promoting *myself*.

Despite growing up in a small town of three hundred people in rural Idaho, I was still incredibly shy. I was so introverted in my *Napoleon Dynamite*-like high school that I was bullied. Calling attention to myself was something I never did.

I've been the CEO of successful public and private companies, but when I went into business for myself, I was at a disadvantage. I knew how to promote everyone and everything except myself.

Like networking, "sales" was an icky, manipulative thing practiced by used-car salesmen and late-night infomercial hosts. I didn't sell myself, nor did I want to. I thought if I was smart, a good person, and really helpful to people that I would get paid.

How naïve.

I wanted that to be true, but it was a fairy tale. After the success of my book, *How to Be a Power Connector*—one of *Inc.*'s top ten in 2014—I started getting call after call asking me to speak. I was new to paid speaking, so I vastly undervalued, underpriced, and overworked myself. When someone would ask my rate, I'd freeze, then mention what I thought was a big number (it wasn't) for "just" talking for forty-five minutes.

My clients appreciated what I did. They loved me, and I loved them. But no matter how much I helped, my bank account never seemed to match the value I delivered.

One day, I happened across an article on how to do a soft sales close. It was one of the best articles on how to approach sales authentically that I'd ever read. The byline: Matthew Pollard.

From reading Matthew's other articles and then speaking with him directly, I felt I could trust him. Here was a sales professional who wasn't trying to fast-talk me into . . . well, anything. He didn't want to use people. He didn't want to deceive people. He genuinely wanted to help. He did business the way I liked to do business—centered around connecting people with what they really needed.

Matthew challenged my basic beliefs about sales. For example, what I looked at as a forty-five-minute speech, I should have seen as days of preparation to create or customize a keynote speech, at least two days of travel, and the opportunity costs of working with other clients during the trip. That doesn't even take into account the value of the insights and experience shared in the presentation itself or the one-on-one discussions with participants afterwards.

No wonder nobody wanted to hire me—I was too cheap!

As an introvert, and especially as a woman who was always taught to put others ahead of myself, I instinctively shied away from the question, "How much do you charge?" Here I was, a former executive of multiple companies, and I couldn't confidently answer a basic question about my own business.

Matthew suggested one line that changed *everything*.

Instead of waiting for someone to bring up price, I preempted it by asking, "Now, when you thought about reaching out to me or considered having me speak at your event, I'm sure you had an idea of what working with me would cost. What kind of budget did you have in mind?"

I could feel the energy of the conversation change. Instead of me timidly presenting my fee, all of a sudden, they were trying to prove they had the budget to work with me.

I began hearing such answers as:

"I'm assuming I wouldn't get much change from $X."

"We really can't extend our budget past $Y."

"I know you probably charge more than this, but I was hoping you'd be willing to speak for $Z."

The prices they quoted were *three to four times* what I had been charging. Best of all, I didn't feel icky. I didn't feel deceptive. I didn't feel that I had somehow cheated these people out of their money. It was pretty validating, to be quite honest.

Barbara Jordan said, "If you're going to play the game properly, you'd better know every rule." I was in the game, helping everyone win . . . except myself. Matthew showed me the rules I'd missed. I learned how to sell my skills while still feeling as genuine, authentic, and helpful as I had before reading that article . . . except now, I also feel like I'm winning, too.

In short, Matthew's sales system pulled everything together and handed me my dream business. Trust his process, and see what it can do for you.

—Judy Robinett, author of *How to Be a Power Connector*

1

when introverts fail at sales

In the modern world of business, it is useless to be a creative, original thinker unless you can also sell what you create.

—**DAVID OGILVY**, *Confessions of an Advertising Man*

Alex Murphy's dream-come-true was fast becoming a nightmare.

With financing from two family members, he had set up his own videography studio. Professional-grade cameras, cutting-edge software, boom mics, an impressive roster of talent—Golden Arm Media had everything going for it.

Except sales.

As the owner and face of the business, that fell to Alex. Unfortunately, like many people who begin with subject matter expertise and then create a business out of it, he didn't have a knack for sales. In fact, as an introvert, he kind of hated it.

After junior high, he had developed a pronounced stutter, resulting in a lack of confidence. Since he was already somewhat shy, this only increased his natural aversion to casual conversations with strangers. His discomfort with social situations persisted through high school and college as well.

Fast-forward a few years to Alex starting his videography business from scratch. It wasn't an established business with an existing customer base. He didn't come out of another business with a portfolio of client projects or an extensive network of people and businesses to tap. He had to build his client roster from the ground up.

So if we're taking inventory: a natural introvert with a stutter (made worse during times of stress)...with an aversion to creating small talk (a normal trait of introverts)...a skewed self-perception and the lowered self-confidence resulting from it...who faces the challenge of forming new relationships that comes from all those factors...puts himself in a situation where his livelihood depends on being able to sell intangible services...to complete strangers. Sounds like a recipe for disaster, doesn't it?

It was.

When he got on the phone or in front of potential clients, he didn't know what else to do but talk about videography and business. If they tried to make small talk or if they happened to share something personal, Alex would just simply clam up. There was a long, unnatural pause while both sides figured out how to get out of the conversational sand trap they'd somehow stumbled into.

We often say, "People do business with people they like." Having spent hours with Alex myself, I know he's a likable guy. But in a sales situation, he had a hard time getting over the hurdle of creating basic rapport with the potential client, much less establishing the necessary trust to persuade them to buy a customized professional service like videography.

So sales sucked.

THE PROBLEM WITH INTROVERTS

We introverts live in a world (or, at least, in Western culture) that looks up to people who act like extroverts. (Even though a little digging shows that *extravert* is actually correct, *extrovert* is the far more common spelling. I've chosen to stick with it for convenience's sake.) We often describe the leaders we admire as outgoing, charming, and charismatic. Successful people look and act extroverted. Therefore, extroverts are the people we believe we should model.

That doesn't work for introverts like you and me. It goes against who we are, how we're wired, and how we think. Sure, we can pretend to be extroverts and learn the tricks that mask our introversion, but at the end of the day, we can't escape our DNA. Asking a hard-core introvert to get excited about working the room is like hiring a performing artist to get excited about accounting: It's just not in their nature.

Carl Jung defined introverts as being inwardly focused while extroverts are outwardly focused. In another explanation, he described how these two types of people draw their energy: introverts from being alone; extroverts from people. In practice, that means an introvert can spend energy networking a crowd or performing for an audience, but we recharge our batteries primarily from being alone. Extroverts, on the other hand, can work in isolation, but they recharge from going out with a group of friends or being in a crowd of people.

Take me, for example. I may look like an outgoing extrovert on-stage and afterward while staying for questions or workshops, but once I get home, I turn my phone off and TV on, sit by myself for a few hours—no other lights or noise—and zone out to recharge my batteries. While I love helping people, the act of interaction depletes my energy. Contrast this to some of my extroverted colleagues who get a rush from being on-stage and then look forward to spending a night out on the town.

Speaking directly to Alex's situation, those who've studied introversion point out that we often hate chitchat and small talk, preferring to talk about things that matter, or "meaningful conversations," as many put it. Who cares about who won the game last night when you're there to get a job done?

One telltale trait of introverts is what some experts call "reflecting internally." It means that introverts do a lot more thinking before they speak. I have one coaching client who often takes so long to answer a question that we had to switch to Skype so I could tell the difference between him thinking and the call dropping. Extroverts, on the other hand, more commonly just "think out loud." For us, though, our aversion to small talk comes across as being awkward, shy, uncaring, antisocial, or downright rude. We're not. That's just how it looks.

Alex, however, didn't see himself as any of those things. In his mind, he was just getting down to business. That's why he was there, after all. He didn't quite know what to do with clients talking about their child's recital or their plans for the weekend. Those things were ultimately inconsequential in a meeting about videography. It was almost as if Alex was trying to have one conversation while the person on the other side of the desk was having another. Getting through the sales meeting often became an awkward dance for both parties.

Once Alex had gathered all the information he needed and

left the potential clients, he'd go back to his office and spend hours creating a proposal, sometimes as long as thirty pages. As soon as he was done, he'd excitedly email it to them. Then he'd wait for days, weeks, or even months to hear back—only to find out they had gone with someone else.

He watched as his dream circled around the drain. The few clients he did land never quite covered the bills. His start-up funds were rapidly dwindling. He had borrowed from his father and maxed out his wife's credit cards—both of whom also worked for him. If his business failed, it would not only wreck their finances but also cause them to lose their livelihood. If something didn't change fast, he was looking at the same hard realities facing nearly every failing business: unpaid bills, lay-offs, and ultimately closing the doors for good. His wife, Sarah, later shared with me that because of the overwork and lack of results, she was shutting down emotionally. In her own words, "It was just an awful, awful place to work."

To say Alex was desperate would be an understatement.

Of course, that desperation only fed back into the downward spiral. The harder things were, the more anxious he got about each potential project. If you've been on the other side of the table, you know what it's like to interact with a salesperson who reeks of desperation. When prospects smell it, they sometimes try to take advantage of it by negotiating for a lower price or more deliverables (or both). Most of the time, though, it makes them uncertain, leaving them wondering if the salesperson will be able to deliver.

Does the service provider lack confidence because they are desperate or because they're out of their comfort zone? If they're desperate, then they must not be very good, right? Nobody wants to do business with someone who's failing. Nobody likes dealing with a salesperson who's practically begging for the sale. If they're out of their comfort zone, it must mean that they don't have much experience, right? We want to place our bet on those who have proven themselves (and who will still be there come tomorrow).

Alex was referred to me by a mutual friend who'd just met him. I saw his work and was impressed by his talent, but not his salesmanship. I have a soft spot for small businesses like his. While I like working with corporate clients, I know that all I'm doing is helping a successful enterprise become even more successful. It's just not as soul-enriching as working with a small-business owner, where I know that my work could potentially change a life. There's something heroic about people with enough skill, passion, talent, and belief in themselves to launch a business. It kills me to see those entrepreneurs fail at their dreams. I've watched mom-and-pop stores open, only to see the seats and aisles in these businesses go empty for a long time before they eventually shutter their stores. I've seen tradesmen with their equipment sitting idle in the garage, or home-based professionals with their calendars sitting empty, before having to go back to their old employer. I think of how stressful it is on a family: life savings lost, loans due, dreams crushed, divorce. In fact, I saw this happen to a friend's family when I was young. His parents saved every nickel to pursue their dream of opening a restaurant. I remember the excitement of the grand opening and how bright the future seemed. About a year in, I noticed that his parents didn't get along as well. A few months later, they closed the restaurant and eventually got a divorce. His dad moved to another city, and I was able to see my friend only half as much. A small business has the potential to completely change your life—for better or for worse.

Despite a great product or service, clients and customers who love them, and people who pour their heart and soul into their venture, why do so many of these endeavors go under? They'll tell you their number one problem is the same as any other business's: They can't get enough clients or they need more customers.

After selling to solo entrepreneurs and enterprises, after consulting with founders and C-level execs, after founding a few multimillion-dollar businesses, and after creating and running the now-nationwide Small Business Festival—which I'm proud to say *Inc.* listed as a "top 5 must-attend" conference for small businesses—I'll share with you something that you might already know or suspect in your heart of hearts: The introvert's roadmap to success doesn't look like that of an extrovert.

We're different and we should embrace that.

WHAT HAPPENS WITHOUT SALES

Red Motley said, "Nothing happens until someone sells something." I have to disagree, Red: Plenty happened to me precisely because someone didn't sell something.

Because of a visual disability misdiagnosed as dyslexia, I graduated high school with the reading speed of a sixth grader.

That, combined with braces and chronic acne, left me horribly shy and unsure of what I wanted to do with my life. Instead of going to uni (you Americans would say "college") after graduation, my dad advised me to take a year off and get a job instead. After a year out in the real world, I'd have a better idea of what I wanted to do for a career and, therefore, what I should study.

A couple of months before high school graduation, I found a weekend job about fifteen minutes down the road in Melbourne working as a part-time assistant for John (many names herein have been changed to avoid embarrassment). He'd formerly been an engineer for the manufacturer Caterpillar but had been retrenched (aka laid off). Afterward, he became a real estate agent working with a large agency called Elders, first in the company's Kilmore office and then opening its new branch in Craigieburn.

I wasn't the person out front speaking with customers. I was the guy in the back doing paperwork with a look on my face that said, "Please, please don't talk to me." I wanted to remain invisible; the thought of selling to customers scared me witless.

With nowhere else to go, though, it was possible that this might be my livelihood for some time, so I studied everything John did. I'd always had something of an entrepreneurial streak, so it was neat to watch a new branch office being set up. I observed John go back and forth with the property manager to negotiate his rent, set up the utilities, and begin to work on the office itself.

Contractors came to bid on remodeling the space, which

included building partition walls. After looking at their quotes, John decided that he could save money by doing the work himself. He was an engineer, after all. He spent months building the walls, painting, moving furniture, arranging the office, making sure the signage was perfect, and getting all the details just right. In fact, he often came into the office in overalls instead of a suit, so prospects usually mistook him for a construction contractor. When he introduced himself as the real estate agent, it wasn't long before they showed themselves to the door.

After weeks of this, one day John walked in and said, "Okay, it's time for us to drum up some business." I wanted to say that that wasn't my job, but I reluctantly got in the car. While heading out to a neighborhood, I could feel my angst growing, thinking to myself the whole time, *Oh my god, he's going to make me talk to people.*

The extent of it was us driving to one neighborhood, parking the car, and dropping flyers into mailboxes (which I've since learned is a federal offense here in the United States). We didn't even knock on any doors, much less attempt to talk to anyone. I still remember forty-five minutes in, John saying, "Okay, that's about enough for the day. Time for lunch."

As a fresh-faced kid who knew next-to-nothing about business, I had no idea how sales happened. I was so relieved; all we had to do was play mailman!

Apparently, an educated professional engineer didn't know much about sales, either. In a short space of time, the Craigieburn office was shut down and John turned out.

He went on to find another job, but what about his up-and-coming office assistant? What happened to the high school student who wasn't going to uni and had nothing else lined up? What happened to his plans of spending a year to find himself before going to college? I'll tell you what happened to him: He was left with zero ideas, zero contacts, zero skills, and zero options. That's what happens when your livelihood depends on someone else...and that person fails to sell.

The result: People get hurt and dreams die.

THE MYTH OF THE SALESMAN

Looking back, though, I can easily see now why John failed. He simply wasn't a salesman. He was a typical engineer: an introverted, analytical problem solver. Nothing he learned could have possibly prepared him for selling real estate services to homeowners. Going out to meet new people and drumming up business was simply not in his nature.

It's not that he wasn't smart; obviously, he was. He wasn't lazy. But rather than focus on sales, he focused on doing things he was already good at. You could say that he was trying to save money by doing the work himself, but the truth was he hid from doing something that made him uncomfortable. Instead, he did what we all tend to do: gravitated to what he knew well. What's more, for introverts, the thought of selling their services isn't just unpleasant; it can be downright terrifying. Many of the introverts I work with can relate. They like doing what they're good at, and they hate doing what makes them uncomfortable (as do most people).

So, they concentrate on the work. Business owners often go into business for themselves because they're great at their functional skill. Lawyers start their own firms because they know the law. Electricians start their own electrical contracting companies because they're good electricians. IT professionals start their own consultancy business because they're proficient with a specific platform.

But just because you're good at something—or even great at it—doesn't mean that customers will automatically show up at your door. Even if you pour money into advertising (usually not the best solution to your sales problem), you still have to speak to people when they walk in or call you up. Marketing may turn up an interested prospect, but there's still a gap between the customer knowing what you do and actually wanting to buy from you. You still have to sell.

Of course, the problem is that lawyers, electricians, and consultants aren't salespeople; they're lawyers, electricians, and consultants. To them, sales is something done by salespeople.

These smart people can learn how to balance the books (like a bookkeeper would), how to hire and train employees (like a human resources professional would), and how to address customer complaints (like a customer service representative would). But for some reason, these same brilliant business owners don't think they can be taught how to sell (like a salesperson would).

That's because they believe that learning the law or electrical maintenance is a skill, whereas sales is a personality type. To be successful at sales, you have to be charismatic. You have to be outgoing. You have to know how to schmooze and how to work a room. You have to be likable. Sales is something where "you either have it or you don't."

That's the myth so many introverts buy into. They give up on sales before they even begin. They think that because of their personality, they're not good at selling. So instead of learning how, they plow their time and effort into getting better at their functional skill and pour money into advertising, hoping those two things will somehow magically close the gap. "Build it and they will come" may work in the movies, but if that's your strategy in business, you're just counting the days till you close your doors.

Here's another myth. What's the number one problem small businesses cite time and time again? They'll tell you it's finding customers. However, after working directly with so many entrepreneurs and professionals, in industries from writing to real estate to personal training, what I've discovered is that finding customers isn't really the problem. Business owners often have their head in the sand: They don't want to meet people, to network, to attend events, to get on the phone, or to set up meetings. They don't see the value in contacting past clients for referrals. And they have trouble qualifying leads and recognizing the ones with the most potential.

It doesn't matter if you're the best voice coach on the Eastern seaboard. If no one knows it, how can you expect to sell to them? These small-business owners and entrepreneurs climb most of the mountain, only to let their dreams die a few feet from the peak.

The problem is sales—but it's so easy to fix!

Working directly with thousands of business owners, salespeople, entrepreneurs, and professionals has taught me three truths:

1. Sales is a skill anyone can learn.
2. Anyone can create a sales process.
3. Armed with these two facts, introverts make the best salespeople.

People go to school for years to become doctors and lawyers, coming out of grad school hundreds of thousands of dollars in debt. I used to tell my sales staff if they would devote just two weeks to learning my basic sales system, they could make six-figure incomes—without the time and without the debt. Frequently, I saw the "this sounds too good to be true" looks or heard, "How can you be so sure this will work for me?"

Here's how I removed their doubt.

KNOCKING ON NINETY-THREE DOORS

When John was forced to close the doors on his real estate business, I didn't try to figure out why the business had failed. I was too worried about what I was going to do. Here I was, just graduating high school, and I had no life plan. How was I going to make money, never mind start a career?

They say necessity is the mother of invention. It was with me. John's failure as a real estate agent left me with no job and no prospects just weeks before Christmas. While the rest of my friends were celebrating the holidays, I was desperately hunting for something—anything—to provide some sort of income.

In Australia, Christmas falls during the middle of summer, so it's summer vacation and the Christmas holidays, all rolled into one. From the middle of December to about the middle of January, anybody of importance is on vacation. Therefore, getting any kind of decent job during this time is next to impossible.

My choices were quite slim. I'd already put off going to college, and there was no way I could tell my father, who was working eighty hours a week himself, that I didn't have a job. I searched through the newspapers (these were the days before they posted everything online). The one and only job I could find was as a door-to-door salesman. The prospect of working in one of these positions would make most people feel dread.

For me, it was downright terror.

I didn't like talking to people any more than John did. Years of feeling like the slow kid at school had eroded my self-confidence to nearly nothing. I was made fun of for the colored glasses I wore to correct my Irlen Syndrome (as mentioned earlier, it's a visual processing disorder, often misdiagnosed as dyslexia) and for my awful acne. I remember one day while playing basketball, the ball hit me in the head, popping one of my pimples. The ridicule hurt more than the hit.

For a shy kid with a learning disability, disfiguring acne, and braces, having my only job option be walking up to complete strangers and trying to sell them phone plans...that was the stuff of nightmares.

I didn't have the oversized personality of those "natural" salespeople we all imagine. I couldn't turn on the cheer and charm the moment I walked through a prospect's door. Back then, it was hard enough to rally my confidence to take the initiative in a group of friends, much less with a stranger.

On top of that, I didn't have the mindset for sales. Despite my entrepreneurial streak, I didn't come from a family of outgoing entrepreneurs. All the parents in my working-class neighborhood went to work, punched a clock, and came home. Going out to find new customers was almost a foreign concept to me.

In short, I was the absolute last person you'd expect to make a career out of sales. But I had no choice: I had to do it, and that meant figuring out how to sell, even if I had none of the ingredients to be successful in sales.

This particular sales company was one of those commission-only places. My manager used to say that they threw mud against the wall and waited to see who would stick. (Not much fun if you're the mud.) Because I showed up in a suit and tie, I was immediately put in the small-business sales group. "Sales training" consisted of three days where we went over the different telecom products and packages "Ozcom" sold. After that, my supervisor told me to go out and sell. That was it. No coordination, no hints, no help—just go sell.

I fully expected that every store I went to would tell me to get out or go to hell. That being the case, I thought it'd be easier if I went where there were a lot of shops. That way, I wouldn't have to constantly get in and out of my car. When I was kicked out of one store, I wouldn't have far to walk to go into another.

That's why I picked Sydney Road, a kind of nearby main street. I parked at the end of a row of shops, stepped out of my car, and looked at the dozens upon dozens of businesses. There I was, in the only business attire I owned, which had landed me a business sales position: a black polyester suit so cheap it shone in the sun, an awful lime green shirt, and a bright red tie. I stood on the curb, looking at the long row of shops, all of which already had phone plans.

I swallowed, walked up to the first one, and had my hand on the door handle when the realization suddenly dawned on me: I had no idea what I was supposed to say! They'd taught me about what I was selling, but they neglected to teach me *how to sell.*

Ninety-two: That's how many times I was told "No," "Get out," "Not interested," or (my personal favorite) "Go get a *real* job!" Ninety-two times I was outright rejected. Ninety-two times I had to swallow my anxiety and try to put on a smile. Ninety-two times I walked out thinking, *What the hell am I doing with my life?*

Finally, near the end of the day, I walked through door number ninety-three...and sold a telecom plan! I was ecstatic. I'd finally made a sale. I walked out of that door with my head held high, already mentally spending my seventy-dollar commission...until I had a horrible realization. I looked down the street at the dozens of other businesses I still had to visit and thought about having to do it all again the next day. And the day after that. And then the day after that.

THERE'S GOT TO BE A BETTER WAY

I find that many people, when faced with a problem like this, will do one of two things. They'll either quit or redouble their efforts. Like I said, quitting wasn't an option. I hated it, but there was no way I was going to tell my father—working eighty to a hundred hours a week just to make ends meet—that I had quit after my first day on the job. I had promised him that I would support myself like he had for us all of those years. There was no way I wasn't going to live up to that promise. But I also knew I wasn't a good salesman. Just buckling down and working harder wasn't going to cut it. There had to be a better way. I had to find a way to make it work.

Now, most people might pick up a sales book to get some ideas. For me, books were torture. As I said, because of my Irlen Syndrome, I'd graduated with the reading speed of a sixth grader. It would take me months to get through just one book, and I didn't have that much time. I needed to make a sale tomorrow.

That evening, as soon as I got home, I Googled "how to sell." I stumbled onto YouTube (then still quite new) where Brian Tracy and Zig Ziglar as well as a few others had posted some sales training videos. I watched until I finally had to go to bed.

The next day, I tried to put some of what I'd learned to work. Instead of ninety-two noes, I had to go through only seventy-two before I got to a yes. That evening, I watched more videos. The next day, I took what had worked for me on the two previous days, added what I'd learned the evening before, and landed a yes at door number forty-eight.

I kept doing what seemed to work and ditched what didn't. For example, instead of pitching to the first person I saw, I would say, "I'm here on behalf of Ozcom. We are trialing out a new savers package in your area. Are you the right person to speak to?" That way, I was talking to the real decision-maker instead of getting thrown out by a cashier.

When I got to the manager, instead of talking about our products, I'd ask for their last telecom bill, then whip out a calculator, crunch the numbers, and show them just how much they would have saved if we'd been their provider that month instead of the other guy. Soon, I had a sale at one in every ten shops I went to—and then one in every five. That is, I went from a 1 percent success rate to 20 percent; I got *twenty times better* in just a matter of weeks.

I couldn't improvise. I couldn't just pick up the thread of someone's conversation and weave it into my sales pitch. All I knew to do was almost the exact same thing every time I walked through a door. I'd created some kind of ad hoc process, and I clung to it for dear life.

When I first started working at that company, the veteran salespeople didn't even take notice of me. They were too busy talking about how saturated the market was becoming and how much harder it was to make money. Many salespeople had left, and even the best talked about walking out, too. I was the quiet kid who sat in the back of the room while they swapped stories, laughed, and slapped each other on the back. But after a few weeks, my name started edging out those old sales dogs. They couldn't believe that this introverted teenager was outselling them. A few even suspected I was somehow cheating.

I began to consistently outsell everyone on my team. In a matter of months, I was the best salesperson in the company (which happened to be the largest sales and marketing firm in the southern hemisphere). Then, the company promoted me to sales manager.

How was I supposed to train other salespeople? All I knew to do was what I'd been doing. So that's what I did: I showed everyone the routine I used. The "naturals" ignored my training and relied on their extroverted personalities. They continued to experience the roller coaster of sales: some weeks went great and others bombed. My introverts, however, followed my methods like a religion. Like I had been before them, they were scared out of their minds; they had no clue what to say to get a prospect to buy telecom services.

Then, a strange thing happened: All the introverts began to outsell the extroverts. Maybe not every day, but certainly every week. An extrovert may have outshone an introvert from time to time when they were at their optimum, but week after week, month after month, the introverts beat their "gift of the gab" counterparts, hands down. Contrary to all myths and beliefs, I discovered that introverts make the best salespeople.

Here's what I didn't know then: Extroverts' sales are directly connected to their personality and even their mood. When everything around them is going great, they sell well. But throw in stress or negativity in their personal life, such as a fight with a friend or while planning their wedding, and it derails their sales.

Introverts, on the other hand, just rely on the system. Regardless of how they feel or what's going on around them, they stick to the plan and repeat their results, sale after sale. Of course, introverts experience the same stressors as their extroverted peers. I remember many morning meetings when my introvert team would share their fights, plans, or worries, but then they'd go out and achieve the same results they had on the days when everything was going well.

ALEX BECOMES A SALES POWERHOUSE

Like Alex Murphy.

Fast-forward more than a decade after my door-to-door sales job. After working with thousands of salespeople and business owners, I had streamlined my process. I had a secret for turning any introverted, shy, or "didn't get into business to be a salesman"–type professional into a high-performing sales consultant.

I didn't originally create it just for introverts. But I found that introverts naturally gravitated to it. I also found that quite a few business owners are naturally introverted, particularly those who own service-based businesses. They didn't go into business to sell. They simply wanted to earn a high income, doing what they loved, how they wanted to, when they wanted to, in a business that revolved around their family and their life (and not the other way around).

Now that I know the numbers, it shouldn't surprise me. Studies in the United States show that natural introverts make up one-third to even one-half of surveyed populations—and culturally, America is one of the most extroverted nations in the world. (Finland is the least.) But here's something even more interesting: Of those surveyed, more than half consistently self-identify as introverts. In other words, there are plenty of people who aren't naturally introverted yet believe they are.

When I helped Alex create his own sales system around his introverted personality, it clicked. I didn't try to teach him sales gimmicks, to be pushy or aggressive, or how to use verbal jujitsu to trick his clients into buying. I simply gave him a series of tasks—a checklist, if you will—that made intuitive sense. Instead of trying to make Alex act like an extrovert (an impossible task, and one that would have made him feel insincere), I helped him create a routine that worked with his analytical, stay-on-topic mindset.

More important, I helped him understand how to continually improve that routine. It would be useless to give him something that worked only for the size of his business at that moment or for only one type of client. In any company, as it grows, changes, and evolves, the types of clients and projects change, too. If I'd taught Alex to pitch only to freelancers needing testimonial videos, for example, he wouldn't have been prepared to do program videos for Ryan Moran, one of the biggest Internet marketers in the industry, or training videos for tech giant Oracle (both of whom are now his clients). You need a system that can adapt as circumstances change.

For starters, I taught Alex about the importance of establishing rapport with prospects. Instead of getting straight down to business, Alex had two or three generic small-talk topics handy.

Let's stop right here. That might sound like the exact opposite of what I said just moments ago. We introverts usually dread chitchat, and as you've already seen, Alex was no exception. Being spontaneous and opening up—even a little bit—is like pulling teeth.

But that's the difference with what I did with Alex: We took the spontaneity out of it. He doesn't have to think of something, to try to find a picture in the client's office to ask about, or to go along with whatever the prospect throws out. By rehearsing three different topics, Alex doesn't need to be spontaneous, nor does he have to wait out those long pauses while he and the potential client find their verbal footing. He now goes into a meeting already prepared to initiate—and, more important, *control*—the small talk. Establishing rapport is no longer a chore or a necessary evil. It's a to do: a task that Alex is relaxed and prepared for because he already knows how the routine goes.

(Ever met a comedian in everyday life? Most aren't nearly as funny as they are on-stage. Up there, they've practiced until their jokes come across as natural—but there's a lot of preparation to make it seem like that.)

For me, my routine became just pushing the play button: "Wow, so glad I made it on time. Traffic was a nightmare! How long does it usually take you to commute home from here?" I'd continue through my routine, hitting pause at the appropriate moments and, when done, pull out the paperwork to sign the sale.

I sometimes pictured myself as the robot from *Short Circuit*. I just selected the right program and typed "execute"; like a computer, it ran virtually the same way each time.

I do not, however, want you to simply rehearse lines like a robot.

Ever see the *Andy Griffith* episode "Emmett's Brother-in-Law"? Handyman Emmett Clark owns a small repair shop and is quite content with his life. That is, until his brother-in-law—a successful, gift-of-the-gab insurance salesman—comes for a visit. Emmett's wife pressures him to quit his shop and become an insurance salesman, too.

The brother-in-law makes Emmett memorize the same spiel he uses. Emmett tries to sell to a couple of Mayberry residents by reciting the speech but completely bombs. The episode ends with Emmett's wife finding him back at his workbench happily repairing a toaster.

Emmett didn't fail to sell because he was bad at sales. He failed because he was forced into delivering a speech that wasn't authentically him. It just didn't work.

I didn't give Alex lines to rehearse. He decided what topics of small talk worked for him, and then he practiced his delivery of them until they were second nature.

That's a crucial point here: I'm not talking about you memorizing lines (like Emmett's brother-in-law did) but rather helping you create verbal sales tools that you can select and expertly wield in any given situation.

In less than twelve months, Alex went from being worried about shutting his doors to being on track to earn a million dollars in annual revenue, working almost exclusively in business-to-business sales. Today, selling is no longer a necessary evil but, believe it or not, an *enjoyable* part of his business.

7 STEPS TO THE INTROVERT'S EDGE

Here's the advantage in sales we introverts have over our extroverted peers: We don't rely on our personality. In the absence of natural talent, we have to rely on a process...and in the long-run, process beats personality. Every time.

In presenting my sales process for introverts, I won't pretend that I've created some revolutionary system. If you're a student of sales literature, you should recognize nearly every insight and piece of advice I present. People have been selling for millennia; people have engaged in sales as a profession for at least a century. I'm not even going to give you a sales system, really; I'm giving you the framework to create your own.

And that's the beauty of it.

With the principles I lay out in each step, coupled with insights and advice created from an introvert's perspective for fellow introverts, you will have the tools to create a sales system that works for your unique business; that you can tailor to your particular clientele, products, and services; that can evolve and adapt over time; and, most important, that is authentically yours.

Let me give you one word of caution: Doing sales this way doesn't work 100 percent of the time. Nothing does. You will have weird customers or odd situations. Even when you've perfected your process, you'll never get every single sale. A realistic goal is to create a system that can routinely lead to a successful outcome in roughly 80 percent of your sales situations. In other words, the vast majority.

We're not aiming for perfection but progress.

Before we dive into the seven steps, though, let's look at it from the thirty-thousand-foot view so you can see how the pieces fit together.

First, establish trust and provide an agenda. "People don't care how much you know until they know how much you care." It's a cliché, but it also happens to be true. One of the reasons *How to Win Friends and Influence People* is an enduring classic is because of how timeless Dale Carnegie's advice is: start by connecting with the other person on a personal level. Even the smallest emotional connection can be enough to help your client let down their defenses and see you as a person (not just a hungry salesperson). If a prospect doesn't trust you at a basic level, then they won't trust anything you say. Without trust, you have nothing but an uphill battle.

Once you've got rapport, you need to chart the course. I once worked with a veteran salesman who was good at establishing an initial rapport, but after that he would get straight down to business. Have you ever been in a class or a seminar where you had no idea where the person at the front of the room was headed? It sounded like they had a point—or were at least getting to one—but time just seemed to drag on and on?

People like to know where a conversation is going, especially in a sales meeting. I teach people to lay out a simple roadmap. You need to tell the person on the other side of the table (or phone) why you're about to ask them a barrage of questions and how it's going to help you help them. It sounds simple, but I never fail to be amazed at how much of a difference it makes for the other party. When they understand even a rough agenda of the meeting, they often visibly relax. They can sit back for a few minutes, knowing you're behind the steering wheel and that you have a plan. And when done well, they understand that what you're asking is designed to help them, so they're happy to answer in-depth.

Second, ask probing questions. It's difficult for us business owners to see ourselves the way new prospects see us. We understand what we sell. For our potential clients, though, we're just another commodity trying to make a buck. Despite plenty of advice to the contrary, most salespeople go into a meeting and, in so many words, say, "This is what I sell. Do you want to buy it?" And if that's what professional salespeople do every day, you can imagine how much more often this crime is committed by business owners and self-employed professionals, especially those who are introverts.

Don't tell them what you sell. Instead, have a list of questions ready to help you find their pain points. Like a doctor probing a wound, you have to probe your client's pain points until you find the bleeding. Then, pour salt on the wound: Frame the costs of not buying in terms that mean something to them. Do they worry about security? About missing time with their partner? Providing the good life for their kids? That's their real problem.

And if they don't want to open up to a complete stranger (understandably), tell stories about customers just like them who've had problems just like theirs. Often, you'll see them begin to nod their heads because they've experienced the same thing themselves.

Third, speak to the decision-maker. Have you ever been in a sales situation where the person was nodding along to your every word? Where you thought, *Wow, this is going great! I've got this one in the bag!* And when you were ready to sign, the person said, "Oh, no, I can't make this decision. I'd have to speak to my [husband, wife, boss, investor, partner, committee, etc.]." I have, far too many times. It's so frustrating to get your hopes up, only to have cold water thrown on them when you realize you're not even speaking to the right person. That's why you need to find out up front if you're actually in a sales meeting or if you're still trying to get one in the first place.

Fourth, sell with a story. Once you've gone through your standard list of questions and found where the prospects hurt the most, help them see how great their life/business/career/relationships/etc. could be...if only they had what you alone can offer.

Sales dogs will tell you to "sell the sizzle, not the steak." The problem is that everybody sells the sizzle these days. And customers are more cynical and more educated than ever. They can compare you against your competitors with just a few clicks of a mouse. So instead of selling them a solution, tell them a story—one of a handful that you've prepared and practiced—of how one of your past customers was like them (perhaps), how they almost decided against working with you but decided to anyway, and how they got the exact result they were hoping for.

In essence, tell them a story that helps them see the transformative magic of the product or service you sell.

Fifth, answer objections with stories. We've all heard the saying, "The customer's always right!" It's useless to argue with a customer. You don't win. Besides, as introverts, we usually shy away from direct confrontation. We don't want to be pushy. So how can Alex Murphy be true to his nature and yet overcome a customer's objections?

Again, stories.

He doesn't tell the customer why they're wrong or how their reasoning doesn't apply. He doesn't pressure them into a sale or try some gimmick to misdirect them. He simply tells a story—again, prepared beforehand so that it comes across naturally—of a customer who had a similar objection or issue. "But then," Alex begins, and goes into the part of the story where those fears or concerns were dealt with and describes the great results the client experienced because of their decision.

You could argue using logic and facts, but that's not a position you want to be in with your prospects. Ever heard the saying, "Win the fight, lose the sale"? You want to disarm them, to help them put their defenses down. Telling a story shifts the conversation from yes/no to "This is what happened when..." and the takeaway. You're addressing their concerns without telling them that they're wrong. They can disagree with logic, they can disagree about the outcome they believe they'll have, but they can't disagree with the outcome of the person in *your* story.

Sixth, take their temperature. Traditional sales techniques say you have to "ask for the sale." While I agree that's the right way to go for some people, I also know that such a direct question can immediately put people on their guard. They don't want to feel that you're pushing them to make a decision. And again, as an introvert, I just don't like asking. I don't want to act aggressive; it makes me feel uncomfortable. It's just not in my nature.

Instead, I use the trial close. For Alex, we came up with a casual question, such as, "So, would package A or B work better for you?"

Now, if they were immediately resistant, Alex could say, "No, no, I just need to explain the exact process we will follow and how everything will work, and to do that I need to know what direction would be best for you." This would often make the prospects feel like *they* had jumped the gun, and they would feel obligated to listen further. It also showed Alex that he wasn't ready for the sale yet and that he needed to describe his services more, ask more questions, and tell more stories before trying a different trial close. With this process, the prospects didn't have to put their guard up because Alex was only trying to "understand."

If, on the other hand, they respond positively, then Alex knows that they are okay to go ahead with the sale. It's an easy way to let the clients tell him whether they're ready or not, and it takes all the pressure off of Alex to be a pushy salesman.

Seventh, assume the sale. Even when I felt like I had the deal (i.e., after a successful trial close), I still didn't like to ask for the sale. In my door-to-door telecom days, I just began to act like I already had it. After seeing they were ready, I'd say, "Now, I just need to ensure you qualify for this package: Do you have an ABN?" (The Australian equivalent of an employer identification number—the company's social security number, so to speak.) When they'd say yes, I'd say, "Fantastic. Would you mind grabbing that for me?"

They never had it right where we were sitting, so they'd have to leave to go get it. When they came back into the office, I was already filling out their paperwork. Yes, it really was that easy.

In essence, I never gave them the opportunity to say no. Once the trial close showed me they were ready, I just assumed they wanted to move forward. I gave them an easy way to say yes, a task to take the next step, and then I assumed the sale unless they said otherwise.

Lastly, but most important, perfect the process. This is really the cornerstone of my entire approach to sales. Whereas most sales pros concentrate on trying to win every individual sale, I take a different tack.

I see sales like a factory production line. When the factory first starts production, the first few widgets off the line will probably be awful. As the engineers and operators tweak the process, though, the quality of the widgets gets better and better. At some point, the line will be running at maximum efficiency. Even then, statistical quality control says that the widgets won't be identical. There will be an acceptable range of deviation from the baseline. Widgets outside that range will be discarded. Smart engineers will continue to fiddle with the line but change only one thing at a time. They'll try different speeds, different line operators, and different input materials to see if each change increases or decreases the overall quality of the widgets.

When Alex goes into a sales meeting, he's not focused on the individual sale, any more than an engineer focuses on an individual widget. Like the engineer, Alex takes the broad view: How well is the overall *system* performing?

He expects that a certain percentage of sales calls won't lead to a sale. He *expects* to fail. The difference from before is that he knows it's a natural part of his sales production line: X number of widgets will be defective; X number of meetings will go bust.

So Alex doesn't try to win every sale. He tries to improve his sales system. If he improves his sales factory, so to speak, then the results will take care of themselves.

Regardless of the outcome, after every sales meeting, he picks it apart. Did he adhere to his process? Did something unexpected come up? Did he discover a new objection for which he should prepare a story? Did they laugh at his jokes? Does he need to practice the delivery of a certain line? How did the prospect seem to react to X, Y, and Z? If he tried something different this time, did it seem to pay off?

He's constantly experimenting and improving his sales process. Better yet, it takes the pressure completely off of him; he's just experimenting. Sales is no longer a reflection of his personality—it's an external process.

No wonder he's about to hit a million dollars in sales. More important, though, he's got his confidence back. He's not worried about whether or not Golden Arm Media is about to close its doors. He's living his dream.

But it's one thing to get people to buy a telecom plan costing hundreds of dollars or a professional service costing thousands. I want to show you how two tech entrepreneurs are using my approach to talk venture capitalists into investing millions into something that doesn't even exist yet.

set the stage

(STEP ONE: TRUST AND AGENDA)

If people like you, they'll listen to you. But if they trust you, they'll do business with you.

—ZIG ZIGLAR

Beth and Amy didn't have Alex's problem of establishing rapport. These two women created tech solutions for *Fortune* 500 companies and were even part of the team that took a tech company public; meeting new people, pushing new ideas, and winning minds over to their way of thinking were all part and parcel of their careers.

They founded an educational technology company before edtech start-ups were even a thing. After getting it off the ground, they began seeking investors to help them launch their platform globally. They ran in venture capital circles and had contacts in the private equity world from their previous experiences. They had pre-existing relationships with many of these people, so rapport wasn't an issue. Their problem?

Trust.

Not in the sense that they weren't trustworthy, but in a "these people don't inspire confidence" sort of way. When they got in front of a potential investor, they lost their poise. They got so emotionally wound up in their desire to land *this* investor that their rational brains were overwhelmed by their fear of not landing the sale (or, to be more accurate, the investment).

It's one thing when you pitch investors on behalf of your employer; it's a completely different experience when you do the same on your own behalf. This edtech was Beth and Amy's baby. They had dreamed it up, created it, and nurtured it. When the product is your passion, it's hard (almost impossible, actually) to completely detach yourself emotionally.

On top of that, by the time they were introduced to me, they'd almost exhausted their network. They'd been told no so many times that they were gun-shy. And on top of that, they were almost out of money and running on fumes. (Ever experience something similar? I have.)

The April 2012 issue of *Scientific American* reviewed a number of studies on the causes of anxiety. Researchers pointed out that any perceived stress, whether an attacking bear or the prospect of public speaking, triggers the same kind of physiological responses. The result: shrinkage of the prefrontal cortex while our body shifts to fight or flight mode. That's the part of the brain that allows for abstract thought, rational thought, short- and long-term memory, "social control," and more. To put it bluntly, when we're stressed, the smart part of our brain goes numb.

This, I suspect, is why the pair performed tremendously in a low-key setting but lost that sense of calm self-confidence when presenting to people who could bring their baby to life with one check—or not.

Half of Step One is trust. Alex didn't have any trouble establishing credibility; he knew how to deliver and could clearly demonstrate his expertise. Beth and Amy, however, sold something less concrete, plus the stakes were much higher—by millions of dollars.

They felt that pressure. This, plus the other stress factors, would play havoc with anyone's psychology. When they got up to pitch, it was almost as if they self-sabotaged. Yes, asking people for a few million dollars is nerve-wracking—especially if you've been told no as many times as they had—but that's multiplied for introverts. In fact, studies have clearly shown a correlation between introversion and anxiety. Extroverts literally don't get as anxious as we do. (Lucky them.)

No wonder two introverts got in their own way trying to win millions of dollars for an educational product that, for them, was more than a company—it was a cause, a life's mission. The people they pitched to, though, were used to hearing that someone's start-up was "the next Twitter." The duo's apparent lack of confidence in themselves appeared as a lack of confidence in their product. They had great media, awesome success stories, impressive experience, and a killer pitch deck, yet they reeked of desperation. Whoever was in front of them was their next final hope.

Not the most inspiring view for a venture capitalist (VC).

Rachel Botsman's 2012 TED talk underscores just how crucial trust is for business today. If you want someone's business or buy-in, they need to trust you. That is, you need a certain amount of social capital invested in a person before you can make a withdrawal of the same. In the world of venture capital, having faith in the leaders and management team of the start-up is increasingly important as more and more start-ups clamor for the same pool of money. After all, the VC needs to be confident that not only can you close them, but that you can also close on the next ten big customers so you can recoup their investment and go on to make some serious money.

Beth and Amy needed to reduce their anxiety so they could project more confidence in the room, stay relaxed instead of feeling defensive, and focus on gaining that initial sense of trust.

THE POWER OF INDIFFERENCE VS. THE REEK OF DESPERATION

We tackled a small problem that unlocked the bigger one.

First, they needed to emotionally detach themselves from the pitch. Easier said than done, right? It's just like landing a job: If you only have one interview lined up, then all your eggs are in one basket. You have to get *this* job or else you go hungry.

The same was true for them. Because they usually had just one investment meeting lined up, all their eggs were in that one basket. If they didn't get *this* investor, then they were back to nothing.

Career books often advise you to never go into an interview without at least two more lined up. That way, you know that even if you don't nail this one, you have more in the wings. For Beth and Amy, that meant never going into a pitch without having another one already lined up. It meant doing more hustling and having more potential "customers" in the pipeline. That, in turn, meant getting out of their comfort zone, reaching outside of their established contacts, chasing introductions, approaching VCs cold...and lots and lots of networking. Not something any introvert wants to do.

However, in those calls, they weren't trying to sell potential investors on the idea of their company. (That's what the pitch was for.) Rather, they were just trying to garner enough interest to set a meeting (for which they also had a scripted routine, aka process).

Even if that meant meeting with prospects more for the practice than the potential, it provided the bigger benefit: They knew that even if they bombed today's meeting, they had another one tomorrow. Plus, they could also casually share with each new investor how well their pitch from earlier that day or yesterday went, or how much they were looking forward to the other pitch later that day or the next. Hardly the "broke and desperate for your money" vibe many investors are used to.

They used to put these investors on a pedestal, but I pointed out that they're just people, too. Sometimes they have fights with their spouse, sometimes they forget to open the garage before backing out, and sometimes their socks don't match. They're just people. When Beth and Amy met with them, I wanted them to see them as people, not as gods holding the keys to the pearly gates.

All of this let them distance themselves from being so emotionally involved in the meeting in front of them. With less worry and anxiety about the outcome of any one pitch, their confidence and natural poise came to the forefront in each meeting.

This tactic also helped them view winning investors as a process instead of a chance opportunity. Instead of hoping and praying that this VC would see the light and write a check, they could treat the investor more objectively. While they still cared, of course, they didn't care as fervently about any one conversation.

It was like finding the pressure relief valve. Once they had more people waiting in the wings and a growing pipeline of possible offers, I could almost hear the steam escaping as they prepped for their upcoming meetings. They were able to relax, have great conversations, start off on the right foot, and start to win VCs over...and it wasn't long before they had *two* multimillion-dollar investment offers.

I used a similar tactic to coach Meredith at IBM. She earned well into the six-figure range, but she'd had the same job for years. She loved the culture at IBM, but she was frustrated by being constantly passed over for opportunities and promotions.

The problem I saw was that she was too worried about her boss's opinion. If he didn't want to promote her and she aggressively pushed, she worried she would be further marginalized.

I coached her to go interview for other positions. Not that she truly wanted to leave, but she needed leveraging power with her employer. She knew that she didn't really want another job, so she wasn't desperate. Without the stress of needing a job, she wasn't emotionally tied up in the outcome. Our agreement, however, was that if another corporation offered her at least a 10 percent raise and IBM wouldn't match it, she'd have to take it. She agreed and went job hunting.

She told me later that if she'd been unemployed or facing a retrenchment, she couldn't have been cool-headed. She would have let the situation affect her judgment. She went into these interviews "indifferent about them," she said.

In no time, she had an offer from ANZ Bank, the largest bank in New Zealand and fourth-largest in Australia, with operations in thirty other countries. ANZ offered her a dream job at 12 percent more than her current salary.

For the first time in her career at IBM, she met with her boss indifferent to his opinion. She informed him of her decision, but allowed IBM to make a counteroffer, if it wanted to. Within one week, she was recommended to the global strategy team and offered a raise of nearly $100,000.

No, this story isn't about how Meredith used my sales process to leverage herself into a far larger role (although she used elements of it). This story mirrors Beth and Amy's in that it serves to illustrate how differently we introverts come across under stress versus when we have options; it shows what happens when an introvert can afford to be indifferent.

THE SYSTEM OVER THE SALE

Forgive me if it sounds like I'm beating a dead horse, but Beth and Amy's story underlines the most important takeaway in this book: focus on the system, not the sale.

Many, and perhaps even most, sales books talk about the tactics you should use while in a sale: "Use words the prospect uses." "Mirror their mannerisms." "Say their name often." "Ask for the sale!" And so on.

But look at the underlying message of that line of thinking:

It focuses on getting *this* sale. It says, "If you don't get the sale, you did something wrong; that's on you. If you do everything you're supposed to do, you'll reel 'em in."

Except that's not true. No matter how good you are, you'll never convert 100 percent of potential customers. I wish I could convert 100 percent of the people who approach me. No one's that good.

But in popular sales thinking, you just shake it off and try to win the next one. You're a knight trying to slay the dragon, a caveman who must kill the woolly mammoth or go hungry.

That's all wrong. What's more, for introverts like you and me, it puts an enormous amount of pressure on us. We know we're not extroverts. We already feel like the cards are stacked against us. Every time we don't make a sale, it only increases our anxiety about making the next one. It's a death spiral.

Once Beth and Amy started lining up multiple meetings, I helped them look at the roster of potential investors to see that, while the odds were low that every meeting would result in securing funding, the odds were good that a handful of meetings *would*.

That gave them a sense of being able to predict that some of their pitches would, in fact, bomb. But it also helped them divest themselves emotionally from the outcome of any one meeting. The noes didn't affect them as much because they focused on improving the system.

This let them emotionally unhook themselves even more. If the outcome wasn't what they hoped, they didn't take it personally. There was a problem with their process, not with them. A rejection meant "You didn't properly sell to me," instead of "You're an awful person with a stupid idea."

That's what I need you to grasp. What I'm sharing with you in this book is not how to land the sale. That puts the focus on the micro. I want to give you the tools to build a factory-like process that delivers reliable results. We're focusing on the widget-building machine, not the individual widgets—the system over the sale.

Or, to look at it another way, we're just running a series of experiments. Just like in a real-world science experiment, you need a series of repetitious steps. You hold everything constant (i.e., you do everything exactly the same way each and every time) except for one variable. You change one thing at a time to see how it affects the results. After you achieve some kind of improvement, you repeat the same experiment multiple times to verify the results.

That's what you're doing in building your own sales system. You constantly tweak one piece of the process at a time—be it a joke, a story, or a question—over a number of sales to see whether it helps or hurts your success rate. Because your customers, the market, and your business are always changing, the accompanying sales process must necessarily change, too.

If something fails, scientists don't take it personally. The failure doesn't mean they're not supposed to be a scientist. It just means the experiment didn't work. They change something and try again. In trying to invent a long-lasting light bulb, Thomas Edison said, "I have not failed. I've just found 10,000 ways that won't work."

Lucky for you, I've found at least one way that does work.

THE IMPORTANCE OF TRUST

I shouldn't have to tell you that basic trust is important.

Except I do.

You know it, of course. Everyone does. But when we go to sell something to someone, we often get so focused on trying to cross the chasm that we forget to build a bridge first.

The most important element of any building is the foundation. If you don't do it right, then everything you build on top of it soon collapses. For example, we introverts often like to skip the pleasantries and get down to business. My dad, an introvert himself, used to say, "I wish people would just cut the crap and get to the point." (Lucky for him, he had a job, not a business.)

Often, we want to fix the problems we see. For almost all the introverts I know and work with, authenticity is key to their whole approach to life and business...but the person on the other end of the phone line doesn't know that. Without first winning their trust, our excitement to fix their problem comes off as gimmicky or salesy. You have to earn a prospect's trust.

In Dr. Robert Cialdini's *Pre-suasion: A Revolutionary Way to Influence and Persuade*, the author rode around with a company's number one residential salesperson to discover what made him so much better than his counterparts, month after month after month. After several sales calls, Cialdini couldn't discern any noticeable difference. The salesman appeared to use the same process and approach as the other salespeople Cialdini had seen. After pestering him with questions and observations, he finally got the salesman to admit his secret.

A few minutes into each sales call, the salesman would say, "Oh, I forgot something in the car. I don't want to bother you: would you mind if I let myself out and back in?" Often, this entailed the homeowners giving him the house key...and that was his secret.

As he explained it to Cialdini, you're going to give your key only to someone you trust. The sales prospects' very act of handing him the key told some subconscious part of their mind that they trusted him. It sounds too simple to work—as will many of the things you'll read in this book—but his commission checks said otherwise.

When I ran a residential sales team, if someone was invited into a prospect's home, the very first question asked was, "Would you like me to take my shoes off before I come in?" It showed basic respect for the home and the homeowner. It didn't matter what the response was. What mattered is that it showed the prospect that the sales rep was considerate. Again, it sounds simple, but one time a salesman named Jude hit a slump, and I told him to call me during his next sales meeting that wasn't going well. When my phone rang, before I even let him tell me what was going on, I said, "Jude, look down. Tell me what you see."

"Crap—you're going to tell me it's because my shoes are on, right?"

He got back into the routine of taking his shoes off at the door, and his numbers soon returned to normal. Again, it's almost too elementary to work, but his commission checks told the tale.

It's also polite to accept someone's offer of hospitality. If I went to someone's office and the person offered me a drink, I always accepted. Always. It seems like a small thing, but it's a thread that connects you to each other. Usually, I was offered tea or coffee. In afternoon meetings, I'd make the joke, "Thank you, but I've already had three coffees in my last three meetings. One more's going to send me over the top!" After we laughed, I'd then say, "But I'd love some water, if you have some."

Today, my go-to is saying that I'd love some water, as I gave up coffee because it played havoc with my mood. Instead, I've switched to yerba mate tea—have they heard about it? That opens a discussion on the benefits of coffee minus the side effects, the sacrifice of giving up coffee, and whether it's worth it or not. I get to share something that I'm passionate about and we get to share the joke about what it's like to give up coffee.

Trust: it's the basis of everything else.

I tackle trust from two angles: the personal (i.e., rapport) and the professional (i.e., credibility). If people like you but don't believe you can do the job, then they might enjoy their time with you, but they're not going to open their wallet. If, on the other hand, you impress them with your prowess, yet they don't feel any sort of personal connection with you...they're not going to open their wallet.

You have to win the customer on both fronts.

QUICKLY ESTABLISHING RAPPORT

As we discussed before, "People don't care how much you know until they know how much you care." Again, it's a cliché, but probably because so many people find it true. The underlying idea is certainly true in sales. In selling on Sydney Road, when I got in front of the business owner, I'd launch straight into my spiel. Without any kind of rapport—without any sort of personal connection—I was just a commodity, a nameless, faceless salesman trying to land a sale. (Oh, and of course, on top of that, they saw me as rude.) When, instead, I began each conversation *as if it were a conversation*…it was amazing. Establishing even the slightest connection on a personal level helped make a person's attitude toward me more positive.

If you called up an old friend to ask for a favor, would you begin by just launching into what you need? Probably not. You'd ask a question about how they and their loved ones were doing. You'd ask about their well-being. You'd ask a question that had nothing to do with the reason for your phone call but showed that you cared about them on a personal level.

Now, you don't want to ask about someone's spouse the first time you meet them. That gets awkward quickly. You don't need to ask about their health. That'd be disingenuous. The general idea here is to ask a question or make an open-ended statement that somehow gets a response from them. At a granular level, the subconscious feeling is that if you're willing to ask a question that has nothing to do with the reason you're there and, more important, listen to their response…well, maybe, just maybe, you're not just a money-grubbing salesperson after their checkbook. Maybe you're human. Maybe you'll actually listen to the rest of what they have to say throughout the conversation.

How can you appropriately break the ice and start a sales meeting without it feeling...well, salesy? Here are some of the rapport starters I've used or coached others to use over the years:

- ► Traffic (as you saw in Chapter 1): "Wow, sorry for being a couple of minutes late. Traffic seems to be getting worse and worse in this city, doesn't it! How long does it take you to commute home from here?"
- ► Geography (if by phone): "I saw from your LinkedIn profile that you're in [city]? You know, I once [lived/ visited/passed through/read about/know someone who lived] there. Is it as good as it sounds?"
- ► Weather (always a go-to): "Wow, isn't this weather [hot/cold/great/crazy]? I don't remember it being like this last year, do you?"
- ► Last holiday: "I hope you had a great [St. Patrick's Day/ Mardi Gras/Independence Day/Valentine's Day]."
- ► Upcoming holiday: "I can't believe it's almost [Cinco de Mayo/Thanksgiving/Boxing Day], can you? Have any fun plans?"
- ► If in someone's home: "Oh, what a lovely home. How long have you lived here?"
- ► If in retail: "I noticed you looking at [something]. Is that what brought you out today?"

(By the way, if you're in retail, don't ever ask, "Can I help you?" We've all grown so accustomed to telling salespeople no that it's almost an automatic response.)

On Sydney Road, sometimes all I needed to do was empathize with the shop owner after a difficult customer finally left: "Looks like you're having a hard day, too!"

Again, I don't want you to memorize these lines. I want you to come up with two or three rapport builders that come naturally and work for you—and, more important, your clients.

When you ask a personal (or personable) question, you go from being a nameless, faceless salesperson to an actual human being. We love to buy, but we don't like to be sold. To help someone treat you not as a salesperson but as something else—an adviser, a professional service provider, a consultant—you first have to take "salesperson" off your forehead. Prospects need to see you as more than just someone trying to sell something.

Have you ever been to another country where you didn't speak the language? Or at least around people who didn't speak yours? A friend of mine once traveled to Thailand. He was standing in a group of people who were chatting away in Thai, ignoring him. They weren't being rude; it was as if he were an object of curiosity. When he spoke a few words of halting Thai, their whole demeanor changed. It was as if they were seeing him as a person for the first time.

This is what it's like when you make any kind of a personal connection with someone. You go from being an annoyance or potential source of tension to a living, breathing, human being. By getting them to warm up to you, you're thawing their automatic defenses. I remember when I was twenty-one, I went into a clothing shop looking for a shirt for a big Saturday night out with friends. (I hate clothes shopping, but some of my pals were gym nuts, and I wanted to look as good as they did—they could wear a ten-dollar T-shirt and look amazing. Not me.) One of the floor clerks took me under his wing and gave me some sound fashion advice. He educated me on what worked for me and what didn't. When we found something I liked, he showed me matching items, explained why they complemented what we'd already chosen, and kept telling me how confident I'd feel out on the town. He helped me put together a few outfits that looked amazing and made me feel even better. I thought to myself, *I've finally found a fashion adviser I can trust.* I walked in to get maybe a shirt and walked out with $3,000 worth of clothes.

That's the power of trust.

You can't blame people for being on guard 24-7. We're all bombarded with sales and marketing messages, from our phones to our Google searches to our radios and even our e-readers. Everyone's trying to make a buck. In addition to all that, we have to worry about Nigerian princes trying to scam us. You know the saying, "If it sounds too good to be true, it probably is." Everyone's wary, and rightly so, which is why establishing trust is more important than ever.

If your intentions are right (and they absolutely should be), you're trying to provide a product or service that people actually need or want. It should make their lives easier, help them solve a problem, make them money, save them money, or in some way truly benefit them. You want to set yourself apart from the pack and show that you're just a normal human being. You're not trying to grab their money and run. You don't want to fleece them out of their hard-earned dollars/euros/yen/whatever. You just want to see if there's a fit between where they are and what you have.

Once you establish rapport, you're already halfway to earning their basic trust. And again, you want to do this in a way that is congruent with who and what you are. You should never have to feel inauthentic or deceptive to succeed in business. I've sold millions upon millions of dollars' worth of products and services. I've never once walked away feeling inauthentic.

The key to that is rapport combined with credibility.

QUICKLY ESTABLISHING CREDIBILITY

This book isn't all about door-to-door sales or cold-calling. However, if introverts can successfully tackle those worst-case scenarios with my system, then they can make it work in less challenging environments.

It used to be that a salesperson was a customer's primary source of information on the company. Today, savvy buyers do their homework online before ever reaching out to sellers in the first place. Deloitte's Digital 2015 survey found that 76 percent of shoppers interact with brands or products before ever stepping into a brick-and-mortar store. Your marketing has to do a lot of the heavy lifting these days.

But even if your potential customers think they know who you are and what you provide...do they really? Can you really trust that they've done their homework and understand the full value you bring to the table, over and above your competitors? I wouldn't bet on it.

Although Beth and Amy had a "product" to sell, they were the ones approaching the VCs. They couldn't assume that the person in front of them had done much background research on them, if any. As such, they couldn't rely on their marketing to establish their credibility.

I'm going to assume something similar about you. If you have a fantastic marketing system, great; it will make what you apply from this book that much more effective. Conversely, you may have an awful marketing system. Or you may have absolutely nothing. (If yours is the latter, don't despair: Sometimes having a bad one is worse than not having one at all.) For our purposes here, let's assume that your marketing is basically nonexistent. As such, you can't rely on your marketing to establish your credibility and earn prospects' basic trust.

Most of us skip this. We're so familiar with what we do, what we offer, and how valuable our services are that we often forget to properly introduce ourselves to potential customers. On the other hand, you probably don't want to feel like you're bragging on yourself. Helping people appreciate the level of value you can deliver often does feel like you're showing off. But you have to assume that the person on the other side of the desk or the phone doesn't immediately understand your value. Until you prove yourself otherwise, you're just a commodity.

I worked with professional speaker Jim Comer, who fell into this common trap. While he did a great job of developing rapport and guiding the conversation, he failed to establish his professional credibility. He assumed that when someone called him, they knew his professional background and his level of expertise.

When they got to the part of the conversation where he quoted his fee, he'd often hear them say, "Wow, that's much higher than the other person I reached out to." He immediately felt angry. In his mind, the prospect didn't value his worth. I mean, he's written for Joan Rivers and Bob Hope, had op-ed pieces published in the *New York Times* and the *Washington Post*, presented on hundreds of stages to thousands of people, worked with *Fortune* 500 companies for nearly three decades—he has an impressive résumé.

The potential client didn't know all that. They'd just gotten off the phone with a person half his age who had three speeches to his name in total. The problem was, Jim failed to adequately inform them of his comparative worth.

It wasn't their fault they had sticker shock; it was his.

But how do you appropriately present all that experience without it being a turnoff? Jim and I worked together to create a low-key lead-in that worked for him. We wanted to present his impressive background without making it seem like he was bragging.

While I can't share Jim's exact script, what we came up with was along these lines:

[After the rapport starter] I always like to know how people found me. Was it by chance the YouTube video of me speaking at the National Automobile Dealers Association? I'm quite proud of that moment: 25,000 people in the audience and, last I checked, 65,000 shares.

It doesn't matter how they found him; the question is an excuse to tell a story that demonstrates he's not working for peanuts at local meet-and-greet events. He's not bush league; he's major league.

Scott, a consultant I worked with, made this more explicit. After a little chitchat, he'd outline the meeting's agenda for the potential client and then, after some initial questions, he'd say, "I'd like to tell you about some of the clients like yourself that I've had the opportunity work with..."

When he got to that part of the discussion, he'd say:

Okay, that gives me a great idea of where you're coming from. You sound exactly like the type of client I work with. I'm not sure if you saw this on my website: I've had the great fortune of working with high-level clients across many diverse industries such as Microsoft, Macy's, Porsche, and Starbucks. I must say I love that I get to meet and work with such an elite group of exceptional people.

He'd go on for just a minute or so, but in doing this, he firmly established that he worked with upper-echelon types. It sent the signal that he was a serious player and respected by the experts he worked with.

Before introducing this into his sales meetings, Scott experienced similar reactions to Jim when he presented his high price: "Wow, I'm in the wrong business." "Oh, um, okay. Does that come with any guarantees?" Or, worst of all, "Okay, let me think about that and get back to you." That last line inevitably leads to the torture of back-and-forth voice mails and emails, only to never close the deal. Ugh.

Once Scott began establishing his credibility up front, even if he was still outside of the person's budget, the responses were markedly different: "Wow, I wish I could afford you!" Or, "That seems reasonable. It's just a bit beyond what we're able to do right now," or, "Okay, let me try to figure something out and get back to you." His favorite: "*[under their breath]* Man, I really want this."

But he'd also hear the answer he was looking for more often: "Sounds great, let's do it." "Perfect. Do you have a contract I can look at?" Or, "Okay, let me talk to my partners and convince them, too."

Do you see the difference? It goes from them wondering, *Is this guy really worth this much?* to, *Wow, this guy is the real deal! Hope I can afford him!* It gives the potential customer clues on how to accurately peg your worth, instead of the customer simply relying on their often ill-informed idea of how much something should cost.

Yes, I know quiet and shy people often don't like to draw attention to themselves, especially explicitly. You don't have to stand on a soapbox and list your impressive accomplishments. All you need to do is find a way to hint at your professional experience. Do it quickly, but do it well.

- ► Offer to send them something: "Before I forget, let me get your email address and I'll send you a newspaper article on our recent award-winning design for the downtown convention center."
- ► Ask how they found you (à la Jim Comer).
- ► Refer to something they read on your website: "As you probably read on my testimonial page…"
- ► Mention a high-level meeting you were recently in: "You know, when I met with the regional director for Capital One a few weeks ago, she thought the market…"
- ► Apologize for being a little off your game because of the big trip or impressive project you just wrapped up.

Again, you don't need to send your résumé. You just want to clue them into the fact that you're definitely not the lowest bidder, that you know your stuff, that you're a professional, and that you're not desperate.

NO HIDDEN AGENDA

My approach to sales isn't about parroting what successful people have done. It's about learning how and why they did it so that you can translate it into something that works for your specific market.

Remember Jude who always forgot to take his shoes off? He was great at establishing rapport and demonstrating basic business competence. After that, though, he struggled through the sale. Prospects acted guarded, defensive, closed. Each conversation started off so warmly, it perplexed him why they began to freeze up soon afterward. He chalked it up to people's basic distrust of salespeople.

I sat with him through a couple of sales and identified the disconnect. After the initial banter and establishment of credibility, Jude began asking probing questions (Step Two) to help him identify the customer's pain points. Like any salesperson worth his salt, Jude wanted to sell the person what they truly needed *and* frame it in the way that best appealed to them (Step Four).

But the customer didn't know that.

All they saw was a total stranger who went from charmer to interrogator. He asked questions about their business, their expenses, and more—information they would never want their competitors to know. Why should they volunteer all of that to some random salesman? Where was he going with all this?

I said, "Look, mate, it's not that they don't trust you. It's just that you haven't given them a reason to trust you enough. They have no context for why you need these specific details. You know what you're aiming at—that you're trying to make their business more profitable and efficient—but they have no idea."

The line we came up with was:

Now, I'm going to need to ask you a few questions about your phone usage and how your business operates. That way, I can tailor a solution that best suits your needs. Is that okay?

By giving them this simple outline of an agenda, his customers had a frame of reference for his questions. Instead of being immediately defensive, they could see that he was actually trying to figure out how to best help them.

Just as important, by asking, "Is that okay?" he got them to grant him permission for the coming barrage. Instead of being the passive recipient of his questions, they subconsciously engaged as a participant in the Q&A. Of course, no one ever said no. They no longer felt "sold to"; they instead saw Jude as a knowledgeable consultant offering a customized solution.

Better yet, this nips a problem we all have in the bud. You've been in a meeting where you barely get started and the prospect says, "Look, how much is this going to cost?" By laying out an agenda, you send the message that they aren't simply buying a commodity: this is a consultation to understand their needs and communicate your benefits, not a sales pitch to see if they'll buy.

Whereas Jude gave just a brief precursor, Scott laid out his entire agenda. After he joked or chitchatted with the person on the other end of the line, he'd say,

> [Name], I'm so glad you called. Before I tell you a little about me, my process, and the type of clients I work with, I'd love to hear a little about you and what prompted your call today.

This accomplishes a number of things. First, it signals to the client that Scott has a process and knows what he's doing. He's had these conversations so many times that he knows exactly how they should go. Second, it puts him firmly in the driver's seat. This is a call wherein Scott's already established an agenda; the client simply has to play their part.

As a result, it allows the client to actually relax. Even though Scott's ideal client is a type A personality used to taking charge, he's found that they appreciate being able to trust that Scott knows what he's doing. Because they see that he knows what he's doing, they can sit back and enjoy the ride.

SHOW THEM THE SCRIPT

In fact, Scott has his sales system down to such an art, he's had people tell him how much they enjoyed the call—not only the conversation, but experiencing a true sales professional in action. This, from a man who once believed he couldn't sell.

Before this, Scott hated sales. He spent all his time working on his marketing, hoping it would do all the work for him. When he got on a call, his "strategy" was to just ask questions and keep the conversation rolling until the prospect finally asked about price.

Today, Scott continues to close $50,000 and $75,000 sales from customers calling him out of the blue. The difference for him is profound: He has a routine to follow, which removes the pressure to "get it right this time" (like Beth and Amy) and, second, he enjoys the sales process now. It's no longer a nightmarish beast to be conquered but a performance to deliver to an appreciative audience. His calm voice, confident demeanor, and optimism about the potential for a sale set the tone for a great conversation...and the client feels it.

This echoes Disney's approach to its theme parks. Disney parks have a specific vocabulary to reinforce the idea that their customers don't come to ride a roller coaster; they come to experience the magic of Disney. Their employees are "cast members," being in the park is "on-stage," being in noncustomer areas is "off-stage," customers are not customers but "guests."

While I'm not suggesting that you dress up like Tinker Bell, I do want to emphasize the point that a sales meeting is often the first true impression a prospect has of you, one that will last for the rest of your relationship.

Set the stage.

DON'T LET YOUR CUSTOMERS RUN YOUR MACHINES

Ever watch *Charlie and the Chocolate Factory*? Willy Wonka hides away in his candy factory for years, quietly and consistently making delicious candy bars. He lets the kids in for one day and everything goes to hell.

The kids loved Wonka's chocolate but of course had no idea what to do inside the factory. They knew what they wanted, but only the little orange guys (Oompa Loompas) knew how to make the machines work together to consistently produce it. Those meddling kids messed up everything.

It's the same way with your sales system. You're creating a

process for an aspect of your business. If you want a consistent result, you need a consistent process.

Who sees how the process runs every single time? You do. Therefore, who's the most qualified to dictate how the process runs? You are, of course.

On the flip side, who's the least exposed to the process? First-time customers. Therefore, who's the least qualified to dictate how your process runs? Them.

You have to establish an agenda so that the sales process runs according to plan. Without an agenda—or worse, by letting the prospect take the reins—you're following them. Their first goal isn't the long-term success of your business or career. You can't entrust your well-being to someone else. You have to steer the conversation. You have to control how things unfold. You have to "run program." It's your welfare on the line—not theirs.

Here's the flip side of that: If you're not leading the conversation…well, then you're not leading the conversation. You've allowed a customer to come into the chocolate factory and start fiddling with all the levers and gears. They don't know how to deliver the final product (a successful sale that both parties feel great about). That's your job. It's your factory, your production line. You're in charge of quality control and ensuring the consistency of process.

Give them the tour—but don't give them the reins.

mine for gold
(STEP TWO: ASK PROBING QUESTIONS)

In selling, as in medicine, prescription before
diagnosis is malpractice.

—JIM CATHCART, *Relationship Selling*

You can find street vendors on nearly every corner in New York City.

They set up their tables, roll out their trunks, set up their tchotchkes and fakes, and go to work. They try to entice every passerby. They want everybody—anybody—to buy what they've got.

On the other side of the world in my native Victoria, Zack owns a business-coaching franchise. Despite the sophistication that comes with his line of work, his approach to sales was less like Jude's and more like a New York street hawker's.

Whereas Jude skipped the agenda and went into interrogation mode—all he was missing was a dark room and a spotlight hanging over the prospect's head—Zack skipped the questions altogether and went straight into the pitch.

Shortly after he answered an inbound phone call, he'd launch into all the courses his franchise offered, the benefits of each, how they were structured, prices and payments, and more and more and more. The prospect would sit on the other end of the line as if in front of a fire hydrant, drowning in information. When Zack was finished, he'd sit back and wait to see which of those options the prospect wanted, even as the person was still trying to come up for air.

Like a street vendor, he displayed all his wares at once and left it up to the customers to decide which one they needed. He didn't want to "sell," manipulate, or persuade the prospects. He didn't want to feel like the sleazy salesman trying to get them to buy. Zack's approach was to present the courses he sold and leave everything else to the customers.

Those on the other side of the line, however, didn't fully understand what Zack sold (even if they thought they did) or how it suited their specific wants and needs. Often, customers aren't even fully aware of what their real problem is. I've had plenty of people call wanting to hire me to coach them or their sales team, only to discover that sales training would only partially solve their problem. After questioning, I may find, for example, that they compete in a saturated market and need to redefine their niche and unified message. Customers often don't know what they need. After all, they aren't the expert—you are.

FIND THE BLEEDING

I'm sure you've read Theodore Levitt's quip that "people don't want to buy a quarter-inch drill bit—they want a quarter-inch hole." They want a solution to their problem, not just a tool to fix it.

Some of my clients come to me saying they need sales training. I say, "No, you don't; you want more customers. Well, actually, you just want to make more profit, don't you? I mean, when you think about it, you don't really care if you have more sales or get more customers. At the end of the day, you just want to make more profit. So let's talk about how we make that happen."

Think of it like going to the doctor. I'm not a medical expert; when something's wrong, I just know that something's wrong. I don't go see the doctor already armed with the knowledge of my treatment plan, the prescriptions I need, and which tests need to be run. I need help, but I lack the expertise to figure out what that looks like. I may even go online and do my own "research," but it might lead me to a false conclusion and a bad self-diagnosis.

That's why we pay for experts: Doctors draw on their experience with past patients to identify potential causes and then continue to ask more and more specific questions until they have a pretty good idea of the cause of the pain.

Your back pain may actually be kidney trouble. Your weight gain could be indicative of a thyroid problem. Your dyslexia could be misdiagnosed Irlen Syndrome.

You want your prospects to think of you like I thought of the sales clerk who helped me select $3,000 worth of clothing: *Finally! Here's someone I can trust to advise me!* You want them to think of you like they think of their doctor or accountant: an expert whose advice they trust and follow to the letter.

It's been years since I called myself a salesman. I'm not; I'm a consultant. I don't just sell a product or service; I consult on people's problems and get them their desired outcome. Once I understand the goal they're trying to achieve—and we both agree on what the true pain or challenge is—then I can suggest some solutions.

Likewise, you don't want to just address their pain. That's tempting because it's an easier sell. But if you're truly going to add value, you need to focus on solving the real problem. If I suffer a deep cut that results in internal bleeding, a bandage only hides the problem; I'm still losing blood.

If you're a student of sales literature at all, this practice should be old news. You want to "probe for pain," right? Discover the underlying cause (aka, where they're bleeding the most) and then implement a solution (aka, find something to cure what ails them).

Wouldn't it be nice if it was as easy as being a doctor and your prospects just trusted you? Imagine that as soon as you asked, "Okay, so what's your problem?" they'd just open up.

Sometimes a customer will do that, especially if you've done your marketing right. These days, thanks to strong marketing, I have calls with potential clients who booked weeks or months prior. I thank them for booking a call and let them know how grateful I am that we get to chat. I then say that while I've reviewed their website and read the notes from their booking email, because it's been many weeks or months since then, I'd like to start by asking where they're at now, what they're struggling with, and what they need help with most in the thirty minutes we have together. And the client just opens up.

But in the case of me going door-to-door selling telecom plans to small-shop owners who didn't need or want to change plans (or maybe didn't care enough to do so), they didn't share anything. The only problem they had was an acne-faced teenager in a polyester suit trying to sell them something they didn't want to buy in the first place.

Door number ninety-three—my very first sale as a "professional" salesman—was a pawnshop. The guy basically bought and sold junk: used watches, old stereos, and secondhand sporting equipment. As I walked in, I thought, *What am I even doing wasting my time here? This guy isn't going to buy business telecom plans. He probably doesn't even have a business phone.*

Nevertheless, I soldiered on.

As it turns out, the owner had been thinking about getting a mobile phone. Of course, he wanted the absolute cheapest option. As we continued talking, I said, "Well, if you're going to get a mobile for your business, then you probably want a 1-800 number, too. After all, no one is going to take a business advertising with an 04 number"—all cell phones in Australia begin with that prefix—"as a legitimate business." He agreed. After a bit more conversation, I said, "Why aren't you on the Internet?"

"Should I be?" he asked.

"Of course you should. You're paying all this money to rent a shop for passerby traffic. Think about selling to *anyone* with a computer! Do you know what you could do? I heard about this guy...," and then I sold him an Internet package. Well, if he wanted to have Internet, he needed a landline. (This was back in the days of dial-up modems.) So I sold him a landline, too.

Do you see where I'm going with this? He'd already been thinking about getting a mobile phone, but as I asked him questions, we unearthed more of his wants and needs. I matched what my telecom provided to what he wanted and before you knew it, I had my first sale.

If I'd laid out the brochure to the junk shop owner and said,

"Okay, here's what we have. What do you want?" he'd have just picked the mobile phone plan. I'd have written the contract and walked out.

Instead, I asked questions. Had he considered what having an email address could do for his business? Did he think that people ever hesitated to pick up the phone because they didn't want the toll of calling a mobile line (forty-two cents a minute back then)? Did he ever use a 1-800 number himself because he liked not having to pay the toll?

I wasn't a sophisticated salesperson. I didn't know how to use questions to uncover customer needs. I stumbled onto asking questions by happy accident in my desperation to make more than the twenty-dollar commission I'd get from just a mobile plan. That's how I walked out with more than triple that.

LISTEN, NOT TO ANSWER BUT TO UNDERSTAND

Introverts are extraordinarily good at listening.

One of the best descriptions of this talent is in the article "The Gifted Introvert" by Lesley Sword where, discussing introverts, she notes:

> They understand the world through careful contemplation and prefer not to act or respond without thoughtful consideration. Introverts will take in information and perhaps ask a few clarifying questions.
> They will not frequently interrupt with questions and

comments as most extraverts are prone to do. Introverts need time "to digest" information before responding to it.

Unfortunately, when we understand, we often want to jump past the questions and go straight to the answer. This was one of Alex Murphy's problems: As soon as clients began to outline their issues, he was smart and experienced enough to know exactly what they needed. He'd jump from asking questions to going straight into problem-solving mode. Even worse, though he listened intently, he didn't empathize with them or make any effort to show understanding.

This ties back into building basic trust: If clients don't know you and don't feel that you adequately understand the problem, how can they trust your solution?

Step Two isn't just about identifying the problem by asking questions. It's also about customers feeling that you're sincerely concerned about helping them, that you've thoroughly understood their problem, and—most important—that you've truly heard them. In other words, it's not enough for you to feel that you know what their problem is. They need to know that you understand and care.

Zack's problem was that he knew too much…as was mine.

A few months after my success with the pawnshop owner, I hit a sales slump. I complained to my dad, "I just don't know what I'm doing wrong."

He asked, "When you first started selling, how much did you know?"

Easy answer: "Nothing. Absolutely nothing. I was lucky just to remember what products we offered."

"Okay, and how much do you know now?"

"Oh, gosh—everything! I know everything about everything we offer. That's why I can't understand why people aren't buying off me. I can explain everything. I'm able to lay it all out."

He said, "Do you think that's your problem?"

At first, I thought that was a ridiculous notion. After more discussion, I conceded he might have a point. When I walked into a shop in the past, I spoke very little about the product and just talked about the prospect of saving money. Now, after acquiring more product knowledge, I focused more on education. I tried to compress three months' worth of learning into a five-minute pitch. It was too much: too much information, too many options, happening too quickly.

Zack did the same thing: He took a decade's worth of knowledge and laid it out in the very first phone call. We both gave our prospects far too much information instead of focusing on only what they needed to know.

In *The Paradox of Choice*, psychologist Barry Schwartz lays out the case that having too many options hurts us. Instead of making a simple choice, we often become anxious and even paralyzed by our desire to make the *right* choice. For instance, two researchers did a study with shoppers in a grocery store. On some days, there was a display table with six types of jam; on other days, the table had twenty-four types. When there were only six jams, shoppers were *ten times* more likely to buy than when the table held twenty-four.

Having fewer options led to higher sales.

Okay, so people buy less jam. No big deal...except it is.

Schwartz points to something far more important: whether you spend your final years eating steak or sardines.

One of Schwartz's colleagues got ahold of financial giant Vanguard's data on a million employees' participation in retirement plans and did some number crunching. He found that for every ten mutual funds an employer offered, about 2 percent *fewer* people took part in the plan.

For something as important as how you spend your golden years, you'd think people would take investing pretty seriously. But the more options people were given, the more likely they were to not make a decision at all.

That's what Zack and I were both doing in our respective situations. We gave our potential customers so much information that they "needed to think about it" or said they were "not sure it's right for me."

Instead of doing a knowledge dump, I went back to asking meaningful questions, intently listening to prospects' answers, offering one or two options, and telling them just what they needed to know to make the choice simple. It worked. Sales picked right back up.

For Zack, I reached back to this experience of mine for insight on how to fix his sales challenge. Instead of laying out all the courses he offered, he took a step back and began with, "Well, what's the issue?" What made them pick up the phone in the first place? What was going on that they thought (or hoped) Zack could fix?

Sales picked up.

FIND THE PATTERN IN THE QUESTIONS

If you've been in business for any length of time, you inevitably start hearing some of the same questions over and over again. But let's start with the hardest scenario: You're just starting out, you haven't spoken to anyone, and you have no idea what to ask.

That's the scenario I found myself in as a fourteen-year-old kid. Except I wasn't selling a product—I was trying to buy my own computer. My parents couldn't afford one (we're talking about thousands of dollars, and my family wasn't exactly rich), so I figured I'd piece one together, using my wages from my job at McDonald's. As I looked through the classifieds, I saw that many stores had the exact same items for quite different prices. Curious, I called up a big store and asked if it could sell me a part for X dollars.

"No, kid, I can't even buy it at that price."

While looking at the other store's ad, I said, "Oh. Well, uh, I think I can. What if...what if I could buy it cheaper than you? Could I sell it to you? I wouldn't want all the money, maybe—maybe just half?"

Click.

He just hung up on me. Yes, that hurt this introvert, but I wanted my computer more. So much, in fact, that I was too dumb to know that what I was doing couldn't be done. Or maybe just too stubborn. Teenagers are famous for both.

Being a nerd, I made a list of stores selling the parts at a lower price, and then a list of all the stores charging a higher price. I began calling the different stores, trying to make this work.

A fourteen-year-old can't hide his voice. Obviously, I was a kid. Clearly, I was a nut. What teenager thinks he can get computer parts cheaper than a legitimate business? I'll bet some of them suspected it might be a scam. I mean, who could take seriously a call that began with a teenage boy saying, "Uh, do you want to save money on your computer parts?" I could see the cards were stacked against me.

But as I kept calling store after store, I saw that different questions got different responses. I began to piece together the questions that seemed to hold their interest. The conversations began to go from "Are you serious, kid? I've got work to do," to "Yes, my business sales do have a lot to do with how cheap I can get my computer parts. Yes, I'd be interested in getting them cheaper."

By the time I got to the fortieth or so call, through trial and error (aka experimentation), I started to build a list of meaningful questions that, when asked in a specific order, increased interest and engagement.

It took probably fifty or sixty phone calls (that lets you know how badly I wanted a computer), but I finally got two managers to take a gamble and agree to split the difference with me in store credit. I hustled, and in just a couple of months, I had enough credit in the two stores to get the different parts for my very own personal computer.

(After that, I stopped. I was too busy playing on my new computer to waste time making more money. Who knows? I might have been the Australian Michael Dell, putting together computers in his parents' garage. Dumb kid.)

Ultimately, what got those two businesses to take a chance on me was:

- ▶ Asking them the right questions
- ▶ In the right order
- ▶ That cut to the heart of their problem
- ▶ And helped them see me as someone who understood their needs

The right question series got me my first computer.

When crafting the sales process for the business training school I founded (the Pollard Institute), I thought that because we offered business education, the question process couldn't be scripted. It was a complex sale, after all. People came from all walks of life and all sorts of industries. But I soon found a pattern: Some questions led to higher engagement and interest, which in turn led to a sale. After eight or nine months, I thought, *I'm being ridiculous*—and wrote out a question series for the sales team. Sales shot through the roof 300 percent, and I never doubted the power of questions again.

ASKING THE RIGHT QUESTIONS

I've heard so many people say, "Oh, I need to ask questions! My customers need to know that I'm looking for their problem!"

Then they ask...and ask...and ask.

They don't seem to have a purpose. They're asking for the sake of asking. It eventually frustrates the customer and wastes their time. How can you be strategic about choosing which questions to ask? How do you put structure around a series of questions that could lead anywhere? Well, for one, you have a set of questions ready. You don't just ask random questions; you ask carefully prepared ones that, most of the time, should lead right back into your process.

I created a list of questions for my sales team to use. It began with saying to the customer, "Now, before we get into the details of exactly what we can do and how we can help, I'd like to ask you a few questions. That way, I can craft a solution that is absolutely tailored to you. Is that okay?"

No one's going to say no to that. Everyone wants something "tailored" just for them. As we said earlier, everyone wants to know that you're actually listening to them, that they're not just another number or another sale. Plus, we politely asked for their permission to move forward. We weren't just bulldozing in, opening up the fire hydrant of information, and then pushing them to sign, sign, sign. We were passive, relaxed, and consultative. You know—introverts.

For Zack, his first question would simply be, "What are the biggest problems in your business right now?"

After he listened to the answer, I had him say, "I can't help you with X or Y, but I can help you with Z. Is it okay if we focus just on that one?"

I mean, if one of their problems is that their spouse doesn't want them spending so much time on the business, unless you're a marriage counselor you probably don't have a product or service that helps. Don't promise to fix a problem you can't fix. (Although you can later use it when you frame the benefit of your offerings. Spending too much time on the business is a symptom of a greater issue, such as a lack of systems or poor time management.)

Next, Zack would ask, "So who's experiencing this as a problem? Is it you? Or is it a staff member who's telling you they're experiencing it?"

If they see it as a problem, that means they are more likely to pay money to fix it. If their staff members are telling them it's a problem, then they may not be as willing to pay for it to be fixed. That is, unless they realize it's a big problem, which might lead to staff turnover, which can be hugely expensive.

When we left off working together, Zack's process was a bit more involved than this, but these questions gave him his basic framework for the eventual evolution of his question series. The better prepared he became, the more he was able to use a decision-tree process: If they answered A, then he'd follow with question #2, but if they answered B, he'd follow with question #4.

Once he knew what they needed, he knew which course to recommend to them. Better yet, he could explain why that course was perfectly suited for them, using their responses as the starting point for explaining exactly how it would benefit them.

You'll recall that Jim Comer's challenge was pushback on price. We developed something similar to this question series for him:

▶ What was their experience like with their last speaker? Were they happy with that person?

- How do they hope their experience with Jim will be similar or different?
- Are they selling tickets?
- Will it be recorded?
- Are they an association or other nonprofit?
- What are they hoping to get out of the conference?
- What are the outcomes they want to achieve?
- Do they have multiple speakers coming?
- How many people do they expect?

With the answers to these questions, he was able to later explain to potential clients why he was uniquely suited for their needs (thereby indirectly justifying his price).

That's all well and good for them, but what about you? What if your business is radically different? What if you're just getting ready to launch and need a question series today? Here are the four basic questions you somehow need to ask. Use them to start customizing the pattern of questions that drives your prospects to share what you need to know to turn them into your clients.

1. **What do they want?** Don't literally ask someone, "What do you want?" That's the internal question that you're supposed to figure out. You need to determine what they want/need before you can determine what they need you to sell them.
2. **What are they doing about it right now...and is it working?** You don't want to be blindsided by offering

a fix they've already tried or are trying. You need context before you can offer a solution.

3. **Who says it's a problem?** You need to know who sees this as an issue that needs to be fixed. If it's not the person you're talking to, their perceived pain will be far less than if they're experiencing it themselves. In short, how much of a problem do they think it really is?

4. **What's it costing them financially, in opportunities, and/or personally?** This line of questioning is two-sided. One, you want to know how much pain they're in. But on the other hand, it's somewhat leading: You want to help them see how big the problem is (and it's often bigger than they realize).

But what if they don't want to tell you what the problem is? Worse: What if they don't even see it as a problem?

GETTING STRANGERS TO OPEN UP

At the Pollard Institute, we focused on a defined niche of clients: tradesmen, such as electricians, plumbers, and other contractors. When we'd ask, "What problems are you experiencing currently?" they might shrug the question off. I can't blame them—who wants to pour out their problems to a perfect stranger who's trying to sell them something?

One time, I met with a plumber who wouldn't even admit he had a problem. According to him, everything was fine.

When I told him that I'd seen thirty other plumbers that month and they all had these three common issues, he said—and I quote—"Well, if they're telling you that...yeah, I have those problems as well." Then, it was like the dam burst: He started talking about all the other problems he was facing, too.

For instance, many contractors have the problem of staff members not cleaning up after themselves at customers' houses. It's a bit annoying. But an annoying problem doesn't really goad people into action. What I needed was to help him realize how much he lost by having an improperly trained staff; I needed to help him feel the pain.

I said, "Let's look at the results of them not cleaning up. Do you always make them go back, or do you go back and clean up yourself?"

He said, "It depends, but I end up doing it a lot."

I said, "Do you get more referrals from the jobs where you have to clean up or from jobs where they get it done right the first time?"

Obvious answer.

"Okay, and how many jobs do you do yourself? About ten a month? And out of those ten, how many referrals do you get? Three to five? Perfect. Now, how many jobs does your typical staff member do? Ten a week—as many as you do in a month. Okay. And how many referrals do they get from those same ten jobs?"

He said, "Generally...ah...one?"

I let that sink in for a moment.

"So let's do the math. Out of ten jobs, you get at least three referrals; they get one. That means you're leaving at least two referrals on the table. Now, how many of those referrals turn into jobs, and what is each job typically worth?"

After he put pencil to paper, he realized he was losing hundreds of thousands of dollars a year in missed referrals. All of a sudden, the question went from how much training his staff would cost to how much a lack of training cost him!

Let's break his problems down into the three costs we laid out earlier:

1. **Real costs:** the wages for his staff to go back and clean up the project site.

2. **Opportunity costs:** the revenue he lost out on because his staff members weren't getting as many referrals as they could be (a combination of not being trained to ask for referrals and not doing the job right in the first place).

3. **Personal/emotional costs:** One time he had to miss his daughter's dance recital because he had to go clean up a site for an irate customer to keep their business.

After that was all laid out, he realized he had a huge problem, one that he couldn't possibly ignore. Thank goodness he had someone asking the right questions to help him realize it.

4

speak to the right person
(STEP THREE: QUALIFICATION)

These aren't the droids you're looking for.

—*STAR WARS*

'd been in the news agency talking with her for almost an hour. She was excited, she saw the savings, and I could tell she was ready to sign. I was reaching for the paperwork when she said, "Okay, this all sounds great. The boss is in the back. Let me go get him."

She walked down the hall and poked her head in an office. "Bill, are you interested in saving money on telecommunications?"

I heard a gruff, "No."

"Alright." She walked back up to the front and shrugged. "He's not interested. I'm sorry."

I'd successfully sold something to someone who couldn't buy it.

Looking back, it's painfully obvious, but I didn't know it at the time: I was so excited someone was listening that I never stopped to consider if I was actually speaking to the right person.

More than a decade later, I made the same silly mistake again.

My phone rang and I found someone from a trade association on the other end, wanting to talk about booking me for a speaking gig. I was just launching my speaking and coaching business in the States. I had my coaching sales pitch nailed after some trial and error (again, experimentation) with multiple inquiries. However, I hadn't yet developed my sales process for inbound speaker inquiries; I still used my basic process. My off-the-cuff pitch was good enough to get him on the hook; he wanted me. I could taste the sale. I was ready to email him the agreement. But in my excitement—and, more important, my lapse in religiously following my process—I forgot the third step: I didn't qualify whether he was the ultimate decision-maker.

Let me stop for a moment to point out that I tell people to always, *always*, have the seven steps on a piece of paper sitting by their phone or computer. I'd have never made this mistake if I'd followed my own advice and had the skeleton of the process in front of me when I took the call.

I realized my mistake when he said the bone-chilling words: "Okay, I think you are a perfect fit, so let me take this to our executive director and get back to you, okay?"

Of course I didn't land the gig. If I'd known—via the qualification process—that I wasn't speaking to the key decision-maker, I would have handled the conversation very differently. Instead of trying to close the sale, my aim would have been to get a meeting with his boss. I would still have wanted to get him excited and see me as "a perfect fit," but I'd have underscored how important it was that I speak to the executive director.

If I'd known, I would have said something along the lines of, "Because of my diverse industry experience—unlike many speakers who just use a canned presentation—I always tailor my presentation directly to my audience. To ensure that I customize the optimal experience for your attendees and to ensure I stay within your budget, it would be great to speak to your executive director before quoting any pricing or committing to a specific way forward. I generally can work with any budget, but my goal is to provide you with an experience that participants will talk about for years to come, and that delivers a real-world, tangible result."

He was the guy doing the legwork, not the guy pulling the trigger. Without me there to communicate all this, I had to trust him to be my salesperson. When his boss ran through potential speakers, I was just another name on the list. They went with someone else, and I bet the speaker they picked was the one who got the gatekeeper to put him in front of the man in charge.

With the news agency, I'd entrusted my whole sales process to the person selling newspapers at the front of the store working for minimum wage. No one can sell my expertise better than I can, especially not an intermediary just gathering information to summarize and hand to the boss. My problem in both instances was that I wasn't speaking directly to the person who had the authority to make a decision.

Instead, I was speaking to...the dreaded gatekeeper.

GETTING PAST THE GATEKEEPER

Some people have designated gatekeepers such as reception-
ists, secretaries, executive assistants, or even digital ones like
email filters and voice mail.

Then again, some people function as gatekeepers without
even realizing it. During my cold-calling days, when I'd walk
into a shop and say to the clerk, "I'm from Ozcom. Are you
interested in switching phone plans?" of course they'd say no.
Regardless of how low they sit on the totem pole, just about
everyone has the authority to stop salespeople from getting to
the boss.

Or worse, not wanting to be rude, they'd sit with you, go
over everything, and then ask for a proposal. I can only imagine how many of Alex Murphy's thirty-page proposals were
destined for the trash before he even sat down to write them.

After successfully selling to that news agency secretary for
an hour without getting the sale, I learned to simply put the
question like this: "Hi, my name is Matthew, here on behalf of
Ozcom, and we're trialing out a new savers package in your
area. Are you the right person to speak to about that?"

It flipped the question from basically "Can I sell you
something?" to "Are you in charge?" Instead of setting the
person up for the automatic no they gave to every salesperson who walked in, it activated another one of their default
decisions: *I don't know what's going on with this guy, so let
me defer to the boss.* Instead of wasting time talking to the
person out front baking the bread, I got ushered in to see

the guy in the back making the dough.

A few years later with the Pollard Institute, I wrote our tele-marketers' script to begin with, "Hi. I'm just calling about a new educational offering to help you increase the productivity of your business. Are you the right person to speak to?"

If they were a gatekeeper of some sort, nine times out of ten they said, "Um, no I'm not. You need to speak to [name]. Let me see if they're available." Even if they didn't put the salesperson straight through to the decision-maker, we had a name to ask for the next time we called.

Our success rate (in this case, measured by the number of appointments generated) skyrocketed beyond the industry average because we spoke to fewer people and landed more bookings...which is an excellent segue into another fundamental principle of the introvert's edge to sales.

DON'T WASTE YOUR TIME

You want more customers. Everybody wants more customers. And herding more people through your doors (literal or digital) will result in more sales. Every salesperson knows that if you just keep on knocking on doors, keep picking up the phone, or somehow keep generating leads, sooner or later you will land a sale.

I mean, look at me. Even a dumb kid in a bad suit knocking on one door after another finally made a sale. I think it was Zig Ziglar who said if you tied your business card to a dog and sent him into the city, one day somebody would call you and you'd make a sale. Eventually. Every sales manager I know repeats the industry mantra as if they were brainwashed drones: "It's a numbers game. It's a numbers game."

Um...no.

As you saw with my Pollard Institute telemarketers, our goal was not simply to speak to as many people as possible. We wanted to speak to the right people. We wanted to spend more time with fewer people.

For instance, if I'd gone to a soccer club and spoken to all one thousand people there, I'm sure at least one of them would have been a business owner who wanted some training. My closing rate would have been one in a thousand. If, instead, I'd gone to ninety-three more businesses and landed one sale, my closing rate would have been one in ninety-three. Which one would you want? To speak to another thousand people before you got another sale or just another ninety-three?

Yet people still fixate on working harder: paying for more sponsored Facebook posts, making more phone calls, spending more on advertising, mailing out more brochures, getting bigger email lists, visiting more businesses, optimizing their website, attending more networking events, covering a bigger area—more and more and more.

Then there are those for whom all of that seems overwhelming so they simply shut down, doing nothing (going back to *The Paradox of Choice*).

When you're optimizing a production line, you want to do more with less: less effort, less raw material, less electricity, less waste, fewer man-hours. Most of us introverts would rather take a punch in the gut than have to speak to an unending line of people, most of whom will reject us before we even get our second sentence out. We want to minimize the number of strangers we have to speak with and sell to.

In sales, we don't want to do more; we want to do *less*.

BE NICE TO THE SECRETARY

With this third step (qualification), that's really what we're after. We want to speak to the fewest number of people possible and land the highest number of sales we can.

That said, we still have to deal with the gatekeepers.

Don't forget that gatekeepers wield enormous influence over your access to the decision-maker. You want to establish rapport with them just as you do with the eventual person you speak to. You want to glean as much information about the decision-maker and the situation as possible, plus excite them to the point that they want to pass your information along. The gatekeeper—be it a receptionist or the sales manager reporting to the COO—may be the one forwarding your email or phone message...or round-filing it. If they're in your corner, they may even advocate for you.

So, while you always want to ultimately speak to the decision-maker, sometimes you have to start with selling to the gatekeeper, especially on inbound leads. With the guy from the trade association, for example, I couldn't simply say, "Look, you're obviously not the person calling the shots. Have your boss call me." That would kill my chances of working with them at all.

In short, sell them on the idea of getting you in a meeting with their boss. Even if they're tasked with getting information, there are questions they can't answer. Explain that you want to tailor whatever you're selling to exactly fit what they need.

You absolutely don't want to attempt to close the sale (because they can't decide anyway). On top of all that, gatekeepers may have their own agenda. The boss might want something they feel jeopardizes their job security or makes them less valuable.

By recognizing that you're speaking to a gatekeeper, you can focus on the real goal: getting through to the decision-maker. You don't want to leave it up to them to be your proxy.

WHY IS THIS STEP THREE?

If you've been paying attention, you see that qualification has often been the first step in many of my stories—figuring out if you're talking to the right person.

So why is qualification listed as Step Three in my sales process?

First, in only the most straightforward of sales meetings (basic cold-calling, such as telemarketing and door-to-door sales) can you get away with quickly bypassing the gatekeeper. Most sales interactions require laying a bit more groundwork before you can simply ask, "Do you have the authority to make this decision?" A sales manager, for example, might bristle at the question, even if her boss will eventually make the final decision. A husband at a car dealership might become irritated, even if it's really his wife who manages the finances. In complex sales, such as enterprise software, you might have to go through several layers of management before you finally get to speak to the top dog.

As such, qualification comes after rapport and questions so that you don't kill the sale before you've even begun. Then qualification allows you to determine if you can go ahead and close the sale or if someone else is the decision-maker.

While working on this very section, I had a great call with a gentleman who had a million-dollar detox tea company. He'd called because he wanted to increase his online sales. We discussed how many online companies used a person to build their brand around. People like to buy from people, not from faceless companies. Facebook has Zuckerberg, Apple had Jobs, Progressive has Flo, and Virgin has Richard Branson.

I said, "If we were going to create a personal brand around your company, would that be you? Or would that be somebody else?"

He said, "Oh, no, that would be my wife. First, she's better-looking than I am, but second, she's super into nutrition and is always really excited about sharing her experience with the world."

As soon as he introduced the fact that his wife would make the ideal spokesperson, it was obvious that she'd need to buy in to this idea, too. That is, I'd just identified another key decision-maker in this sale. That changed my tack from trying to sell him to getting him excited about putting his wife on the phone so I could sell to them both.

I remember joking with him, saying, "She sounds perfect,

but to ensure we're all on the same page, I suggest we set up another call with all of us to plan our way forward together. Plus, if you're anything like me, if I were to make a decision like this that involved my wife, I'd want to check in and make sure it was okay first!"

Being a smart husband, he agreed.

PEOPLE LOVE TO QUALIFY

Here's the shiny other side of the "qualifying" coin.

Not too long after learning that I needed to speak to the right person, I learned how to kill two birds with one stone. I found a way to be seen as a consultant and get to the decision-maker at the same time by using this line: "Hi, my name's Matthew. I'm here on behalf of Ozcom to talk about a savers package that's just being released in your area. I'm just here to see if you qualify for that. Are you the right person to speak to?"

Now, people love to qualify. Everybody likes to feel that they're good enough to get into the club, the pool of applicants, the inner circle, or whatever it is. Qualifying puts an air of exclusivity around whatever it is you're offering. I've even had prospects say, "I'm not interested in education"—or changing telecom providers or business coaching or whatever I was selling—"but I'm happy to see if I qualify." And then they wound up signing.

It doesn't matter if everyone qualifies (as with the telecom plans I sold) or if there are criteria only a select few meet (as with a Black MasterCard). Everyone wants to feel like they're part of the in-crowd.

Now, with your sales process, I'm not suggesting that you should tell every potential customer that they may not qualify to work with you. The principle here, if it's appropriate, is to introduce the idea that they may not be "good enough" to do business with you.

What we're really keying in on here is the "keeping up with the Joneses" mentality, as well as the primal fear of loss. We absolutely hate losing something. Study after study shows that, given two choices, people overwhelmingly—sometimes even irrationally—choose to keep what they have instead of taking a tiny risk for a far greater reward. That is, we're more motivated by the fear of losing something than we are by the near-certainty of gaining something, *even if it doesn't make logical sense.*

Basically, you want to play a professional version of hard-to-get. You don't want to be desperate. You want to raise the question of whether it's even possible to work together. Not everyone qualifies, and the better you get at sales and your business overall, the truer that becomes.

When I began introducing myself this way, business owners immediately pegged me higher than just another door-to-door salesman. I wasn't trying to sell them something, per se; I was there to see if they qualified to buy something. This small change in word choice resulted in a huge change in perception.

If the first person I spoke to was a gatekeeper, the result was the same as before: They'd say no and then go get the boss. They didn't know what was going on, but they knew it was above their pay grade.

They'd go to the back office and say, "Hey, there's some guy here to see if you qualify for something." The business owner would immediately be intrigued and come out to see what they may or may not qualify for. Even better, I was automatically elevated from being seen as a salesman to being seen as something else (ideally, a consultant). Again, very simple, but very effective.

It's a lot easier to get customers' attention by making them feel exclusive or even elite than by being a typical pushy salesperson.

don't sell—tell
(STEP FOUR: STORY-BASED SELLING)

We are, as a species, addicted to story. Even when the body goes to sleep, the mind stays up all night, telling itself stories.

—JONATHAN GOTTSCHALL

Richard Hurley teaches piano to autistic children.

If that one sentence alone doesn't tug at your heartstrings, you must be made of sterner stuff than I am. Once I met the man after an event I spoke at, I thought he immediately qualified for some kind of sainthood. What an incredible mission to commit your life to.

Unfortunately, no good deed goes unpunished. While Richard loved what he did personally, professionally the business was a challenge. In fact, he'd convinced himself that business was supposed to be a struggle—that what he faced was just a normal part of it.

Believe it or not, the problem wasn't finding potential students. Richard operated in a defined geographic location (Austin metro) in a fairly well connected community of target clients (schools, support groups, activity groups, and more for autistic children and their families).

Nor was the problem reaching those families. Email lists, group threads, and sponsoring events put him in touch with nearly all the parents of potential students.

There wasn't a disconnect in people understanding what he

offered. Children have been taking piano lessons since pianos were invented.

Credibility wasn't an issue. Richard had written a book, *Baby Cheetah Plays Piano*, and even developed an iPhone app, Chroma Cat. He was well connected and well regarded in the Austin special needs community. Price wasn't the primary problem; those same parents spent the same amount or more on other activities for their children.

"Okay, Richard, so it sounds like you don't have any issues getting people on the phone or even getting them into your music room. So, what do you say at that point?" I asked.

"I...I don't know what else to say. I teach autistic kids piano. That's what I do."

Again, sell the sizzle, not the steak: Don't sell the feature (what it is), but the benefit (what it does). This goes back to Theodore Levitt's line about buying a quarter-inch drill bit versus a quarter-inch hole. But listing the benefits of an autistic child learning the piano—they will enjoy it, it gives them an outlet, it's rewarding—fails to capture the imagination. It all sounds well and good, but you have to put yourself in the shoes of the parent. Depending on the child's unique needs, introducing something new and potentially stressful into their routine can be upsetting. It's not just the decision of whether to enroll their child in piano lessons. It's a family decision that requires a lot of planning, commitment, and yet more disruptions in their schedule. It's not a decision his students' parents took lightly.

Weighing the benefits Richard presented against the cost—financial and emotional—of piano lessons, most parents chose to forgo the toil and continue with their child's life as-is.

Even for those who were willing to make the changes, it was hard for them to justify the cost. Why was he so much more expensive than the average piano teacher? It's "just" piano, right? Sure, they were referred, but a referral is nothing more than "I think you should try this" or "My child gets a lot out of it." Not enough to sell it.

After hearing this, I told Richard that we needed to figure out why his longtime students stayed enrolled. What was it those parents saw or experienced that made them feel the costs were worth it? But instead of just listing what that might be, I asked Richard to tell me a story.

"Well, they all talk about how uncommunicative their child is and how difficult it is to draw them out. But one mother, after watching her son play 'The Minute Waltz' by Chopin at home...it was like she suddenly saw the real *person* inside her son. Most parents with autistic children feel isolated. They work tirelessly to create a good life for their child, but many people around them think they're crazy. Their friends and family often mistakenly believe that an autistic child isn't fully aware of the world around them. But when he played that piece of music—all of a sudden, there was validation there. Alice saw the human being behind his severe autism. It was one of the most beautiful moments of her life."

I said, "Richard! That's it! Tell them that story! Don't tell parents that it's rewarding or that it draws the child out. Let them feel that emotional connection. Let them experience what it's like."

After seeing where I was going, Richard began recalling other stories: how one student's physical therapist was amazed at his progress and newfound cooperation; how another mother showed off her son's musical talents at a family Christmas party; how a father bridged the isolation between him and his son through sharing the piano.

I said, "That's perfect! Just do this: When talking to parents, ask them what drew them to you. When they say, 'I heard you do piano for autistic children,' you say, 'Yes, and I love to do it. It's such a great experience for both the child and their parents. So many parents feel isolated, trying their best to make a great life for their child, and yet so many people around them don't get it—they think the parents are crazy for putting in all the time and money. But when they see that child beautifully express himself through piano, they see him in a whole new light. Let me give you an example. A recent client of mine, Alice...' and then you tell them the same story you just told me."

Don't you feel the emotional connection? Even for just the briefest of moments, didn't your heart open up a little bit? Can you not see how parents hearing this story would want this for their child? If you had an autistic child, wouldn't you want what Alice experienced? If you had a special needs child and you heard these heartrending stories of how learning the piano had changed these children's and parents' lives, how could you say no?

Do you see how we short-circuited a logical response to benefit versus price and turned it into an emotional driver behind the decision? That's what you need to do. Don't sell features and benefits. Tell a story.

EMBED THE SOLUTION IN A STORY

Here we are, at the heart of the sale.

Everything in a sales system combines to make it work over-all, but stories are the main engine. If you've established rap-port and credibility, set the agenda, gotten in front of the decision-maker, and asked insightful questions, great—but you still haven't proposed anything. You haven't put an offer on the table. You haven't told them how you can make their life better, their bank account jingle, or their mother-in-law love them more. All you've done is figured out that they have a problem you can solve.

- ▶ **Problem:** The parents want more for their child.
- ▶ **Solution feature:** "I teach autistic kids piano."
- ▶ **Solution benefit:** "They enjoy it. It gives them an out-let. It's fulfilling for parent and child."

See? None of that really captures the beautiful essence of what Richard Hurley offers. To capture the emotional benefit, he needed the space to tell a story: a before and after, with a happy ending.

Now, what if you sell weather protectors for windows and doors, like my client Trey? Hard to get emotional about paying for something you won't even notice under your windowsill.

But once you hear the story of one of Trey's customers, you can't help but be moved. The man scrimped and saved to build his dream home. He didn't realize that the windows and doors weren't installed with the proper metal flashing around them.

About three years later, he noticed some bubbling around the trim of his home. He thought nothing of it, chalking it up to perhaps the weather, and just painted over it. After another two years, he discovered that the bubbling came from his windows and doors constantly leaking rainwater down the inside of his walls and into his foundation.

He found out that his home—his castle—was full of mold.

He had to move his family out, hire people in hazmat suits to clean up the mold, and repair or replace the damaged areas. The water damage cost more than what he'd originally paid to build the entire house!

Millions of Americans have been victims of similar misfortune, most of whose homes have been built by professional contractors. Trey himself had something similar happen to his own dream home. After the first big rain, water was everywhere. It turns out that the contractors hadn't properly installed the flashing on his own windows and doors. Trey wanted to make sure that what had happened to him wouldn't happen to anyone else.

He invented an easy-to-install water protector for windowsills and doorsills to prevent the nightmare that he and so many others had endured from happening to other homeowners.

See? You don't have to tell your life story. It can be quite short. The piano story clocks in at seventy-seven words. Trey's comes in at a hundred and thirty. The stories take three minutes to say out loud, yet pack more punch than an hour of simply listing features and benefits.

THE SCIENCE OF STORYTELLING

When I first began using stories in my sales pitches, I could see that they worked, though I didn't know why. Years later, I learned of the academic research (including neuroscience) on the differences between receiving pure information and listening to a story.

The physiological differences amaze me. For example, researchers in Spain found that when participants read words that evoke a sense of smell (e.g., *perfume* and *coffee*), different areas of the brain light up than when those same people read non-sensory words (e.g., *chair* and *key*). In other words, the more sensory the words, the more the brain engages.

Psychologist Raymond Mar's 2011 neuroscience study provides evidence that we use the same parts of the brain to understand stories as we do to understand other people. To translate his research into sales speak: Stories help the receiver empathize with the storyteller and better understand their "who," "what," and "why."

Perhaps one of the most comprehensive approaches to investigating the power of story to move people comes from Dr. Paul Zak, a colleague of the late management guru Peter Drucker and whose research has been funded by no less than DARPA (the legendary Defense Advanced Research Projects Agency). His studies on the effect of oxytocin (a natural chemical that, among other things, helps us empathize with other people) and storytelling show a direct correlation between stories and trust. He's even coined the term *neuromanagement* to describe how managers can use stories to create a workplace culture of trust.

And then there's Significant Objects.

In 2009, Josh Glenn and Rob Walker devised an experiment. They bought or gathered two hundred objects: tchotchkes, trinkets, thingamajigs, knickknacks, knockoffs, and bric-a-brac. They didn't pay more than $1.50 for any one item. Then they gathered nearly a hundred writers to write short stories somehow relevant to the individual objects. With the stories in hand, they posted each object for sale on eBay with the short story as the object's description. They made sure it didn't appear that the story described the object—they didn't lie, deceive, or mislead the potential buyers. Sometimes, the stories were pure fantasy and clearly unreal, like a child getting trapped inside a tiny snow globe.

A plastic toy hot dog in a bun had a story about the seller recalling the fairy tale of Tom Thumb and Hunca Munca finding a fake feast in a dollhouse. The closing line of the description said, "I keep the hot dog to remind myself that food does not have to be beautiful."

There's nothing special about the hot dog. You could probably go to the dollar store and find a whole set of plastic toy foods. Yet this plastic hot dog—bought for 12¢—sold on eBay for $3.58.

In the Significant Objects Project's first experiment, $128.74 worth of junk sold for an astonishing $3,612.51. They did it again. It worked again. They did it a third time. Sold a couple of hundred dollars' worth of junk for thousands (all donated to charity and the contributing writers).

Let's review. The buyers of the plastic hot dog or plastic snow globe clearly knew they weren't buying anything special. They could find something similar (if not the exact item) at any yard sale or thrift store. The story only tangentially involved the object, at best. And yet two hundred people were willing to buy something nearly worthless for, on average, 2,800 percent more than what it originally sold for...all because they read a good story. If stories could sell junk like this, just imagine what they could do to sell an awesome product or service like yours!

CRAFTING YOUR FIRST STORY

You have stories, even if you don't know it.

Even if you just started your business yesterday, you've seen, heard, and read about other people. You have personal experiences you can relate. You have stories from your previous employer. And honestly, to get started, you need only one good story.

It's easier for us introverts to tell stories than to sell benefits. Benefits are a list of things you say that you believe the prospect wants to hear. They lack heart and soul. Listing them feels unnatural and inauthentic. Plus, remembering benefits in order is incredibly hard to do, especially in the middle of a sales meeting. When I tried to learn a list, I'd get tongue-tied and inevitably forget at least one component.

Let's say I gave you a list of three things: food, chair, bed. If I came back in one year and asked you to repeat that list to me in order, you might not even remember the conversation, much less the list.

Yet right now, you could tell me the story of "Goldilocks and Three Bears." What did she do? She ate their food, broke their chairs, and slept in their beds. You have no trouble remembering this same sequence of things as on my list, from a bedtime story you might not have heard for years.

Professor Jennifer Aaker at Stanford discovered that people are twenty-two times more likely to recall information delivered in the form of a story than listed as just plain facts. And Dr. Uri Hasson at Princeton uncovered evidence of what's called "neural coupling": When we listen to a story, our brains begin to synchronize with the storyteller's; the same parts of our brains become active at the same time. Telling a story is as close to telepathy as you can get.

Stories flow naturally. We're all used to telling stories, from the time we fell in the mud as a child to a crazy family holiday. What's more, you've told those same stories countless times. The more you tell it, the better you get.

Think about the story of how you met your significant other. The first time you ever told it, it probably felt a bit bulky. After telling it over and over, you probably noticed that at some parts, people's eyes glazed over, but at other parts their eyes shone with interest. Naturally, you probably started running through the parts where your story got bogged down or skipping them altogether. You might have even started dramatizing or embellishing the interesting parts to make it funnier or more exciting. Do this enough and you wind up with a theatrical masterpiece.

Why should your customer stories be any different? All you have to do is find one or two stories that somehow convey the value of what you sell, and tell them well.

Undoubtedly, by now, you have a voice inside your head protesting, "But I don't want to sound like a robot!" Think back to your favorite movie and your favorite actor in it. You didn't love their portrayal of their character because they seemed inauthentic or robotic, did you? Yet their words came from a script.

You may be thinking that sales scripts are robotic because you have heard telemarketers and salespeople sound scripted. I'm sure that you've seen bad actors do the same thing. But what separates the good actors from the bad, just like the good salespeople from the bad, is their diligence to script mastery. They make the script their own. To achieve this, just like a professional actor, you must start by learning the words of the script to 100 percent accuracy.

You can't sit there and read from your script. That's why telemarketers always sound robotic. They're just reading out loud. A good salesperson memorizes their script and practices it over and over again until it sounds natural.

I had one salesman who followed my training religiously. He recorded me going through the team's script and then played it during his morning treadmill run and then in his tape deck on the way to meetings. No surprise—his sales were consistently among the best.

If you don't know where to start, I've broken it down for you. The structure below gives you a working idea of what to focus on, about how long the elements should be, and the components your story should include.

But don't just tell them off the cuff. This is your livelihood we're dealing with here—the difference between you pursuing your dream and having to find another job. Write it down and practice, practice, practice.

1. **The problem:** the lead-in to the story. Start with where the person was: This was their problem, this was their situation, and this was their emotional state (the "before" picture). You want to describe what's going on so that your customer sees that you really do understand what they're facing. Highlight the concern, personal stress, anxiety, and frustration, such as the fear of losing it all or the hope of connecting with your child. Use sensory words: the rich smell of *coffee*, the wet stink of *mold*. You want them to feel and see themselves in the story with the same pain or desires.

2. **Analysis and implementation:** You want to outline how you went about analyzing their situation and what you suggested would fix the problem. State their *aha!* moment: They now see that they were getting in their own way or that they didn't have the correct perspective on their challenge. Next, talk about what they had to do to achieve the solution— that is, they worked for three months solid. Above all, *do not teach*. The moment you sound like a teacher, you automatically place the listener in the role of the student. Nobody likes to feel they're back in grade school. You're not there to lecture; you're

there to motivate and inspire (like all good stories do) while sharing a moral that speaks to their needs.

3. **Outcome:** Here, you tell the "after" part of the story: They had this return, changed their outlook, lost forty pounds, reconnected with their long-lost brother. In doing so, reestablish where they came from to where they are now: "So Alex went from being underwater with credit card debt and spending hours and hours writing monstrous proposals that nobody ever read to growing his business to seven figures with nothing more than an initial meeting and a few bullet points in an email."

4. **The moral of the story:** why the prospect needs that implementation. Here's where you say, "That's why it's so vitally important to spend time learning the sales process. Many people would've said, 'Well, that's a lot of work,' but when you take into account all the networking events Alex went to in order to get an appointment, going to those meetings, writing those long proposals, and the extensive follow-up—sometimes over weeks and months, and what all those activities cost him, only to wind up with a net result of 'not interested'...if you think about it, it's not a lot of work to learn the sales process, but it is a lot of work to continue to avoid it."

That's important enough to say again: It's not a lot of work to learn how to sell. It *is*, however, a lot of work if you continue to avoid it.

don't argue—augment

(STEP FIVE: DEALING WITH OBJECTIONS)

Tact is the art of making a point without making an enemy.

—SIR ISAAC NEWTON

Thomas worked for the Austin branch of Colliers International, a global real estate firm. His bosses were about to let him go because his introverted nature simply didn't produce sales results. Desperate for help, he got his boss to agree to hire me for an initial consultation to help him figure out how to be a successful salesperson despite—and I write that sarcastically—his introverted nature.

As it turned out, they hired me to train not only Thomas but the other two salespeople on his team as well. These coworkers were "naturals"—gift-of-the-gab, extroverted, hard-core salesmen. They saw every call, every sales appointment, and every interaction as a battle to be won, and the customer's objections, a foe to be vanquished.

One salesman was especially aggressive. He even went so far as to nickname himself "the bulldog." He knew the tactics, knew the terrain, and knew he had to get across the minefield of objections.

Every morning, he would hype himself up on coffee, then pick up the phone and plow through call after call, bulldozing his way over people in his relentless march to victory. He told me stories of how he'd be standing, fists planted on the table, yelling at the phone's speaker to the customer on the other end of the line.

Wow. What a way to live.

I brought all three salesmen together and said, "Guys, try this: When you hear an objection, instead of hammering at them until they either give in or hang up, just tell them a story."

Now, if you're like me or any of the introverts I know, when you hear an objection, you need a moment. You need to think of how to respond. I quoted Lesley Sword earlier: "Introverts need time 'to digest' information before responding to it." We like to thoughtfully consider our answers; we're not usually known for our instant, stinging retorts. When someone objects, our natural instinct is to withdraw into ourselves. That's why we're at a loss for words.

Wouldn't it be great if you could just press pause for a second and ask yourself, "Now which one of my stories would speak to their concern here?"

I have good news: There is a way. I call it the "objection-handling cushion." This is just a phrase that you'll deliver as knee-jerk reaction anytime your customer objects. It's a space filler that's so well practiced, it rolls off the tongue automatically while we mentally catalog the stories in our arsenal and choose the best one.

I always coach my clients to say, "I perfectly understand, and the last thing I want to do is waste any of your time, however..." Then, if the prospect objects with something else, they should use a shortened version of the same thing: "I perfectly understand, however..."

The reason I suggest they use this exact phrase is because I know it works. It's been tested and tried from Tasmania to Texas. That said, you need to be authentic. If this phrase isn't really you, experiment to find something that is. Then practice, practice, practice. You want your response to be instantaneous. That way, your mouth is moving while your brain is working, choosing the right objection-handling story.

(On a side note: Don't ever use the word *but*. It negates everything that precedes it. Imagine someone giving you the compliment, "You know, that looks great on you, but..." They might as well drop the nice part because all you're going to hear is whatever comes next. When dealing with an objection, you want to ensure that the prospect knows you listened; you want to validate their point of view, not negate it.)

For the two extroverts at Colliers, this objection cushion provided an additional benefit: It forced them to stay levelheaded even when they wanted to shout into the phone. For Thomas the introvert, it bought him a moment to ready his response.

Just as we discussed in Chapter 5, you don't want to confront the objection head-on.

Instead, tell them a story. Have an objection story of someone "just like" them who had a similar concern but decided to go through with a decision anyway, and why today they're so glad they pulled the trigger because of the result—which you think is probably what the customer in front of you wants, too.

In explaining this to the three salesmen, I said, "It could be a story about a similar client and how their concerns were laid to rest once they went with Colliers. It could be about a recent success you or your team had. It could be about someone who had the exact same objection and why they finally decided to go forward, despite it. Just tell them a story."

The coffee-hyped sales warrior said, "Matthew, they hang up on me now, and I'm short and to the point—on average, about eight seconds. You want me to tell them a long-winded story and expect them to stay on the line? They'll just hang up even faster."

After more consulting and coaching—in which I told objection-handling stories to overcome their objections—the two sales dogs were finally ready to give it a try. When they heard "It's too early for us to look at that," "We have an agent already," or, "I'm not interested," they learned to squelch their ingrained habit of brandishing their sword and hacking away.

Instead, in response to someone saying they had too long on their current lease to worry about another one, the bulldog said, "I perfectly understand, and the last thing I want to do is waste any of your time. However, we actually had a client, John, who told us the same thing about six months ago. I told him that with Austin's growth, commercial real estate properties are renting out fast, and if you wait too long, you miss the opportunity to take advantage of some great new construction discounts. He decided to give me the benefit of the doubt, and he was so glad that he did. If he had put it off any later, he'd have left hundreds of thousands of dollars on the table. So, as I said, I wouldn't want to waste any of your time, but it might be worth a discussion to make sure that you don't miss out on the same opportunity."

People can argue with logic and facts; stories sidestep all of that. Instead of turning the discussion into an argument or trying to run people over—"Here's why nothing you just said is valid," which just makes you look pushy and forces them to believe you or not—a story addresses their concerns, validates that they have a legitimate fear, and gives them a measure of proof that you've helped others just like them deal with the same, all without directly refuting the customer's claims or assertions.

It's easy for them to argue with numbers or alleged benefits, but it's harder for them to say that stories about your other clients are invalid. Really, what are they going to do? Call you a liar?

It diffuses the conversation and disarms the customer because you didn't attack them or their concerns. You're simply relating something that occurred to someone else and pointing out the similarities.

So how did this work for Colliers? By becoming storytellers, they didn't just hit their stretch goal. Within the first two months, this office—already one of the largest commercial real estate firms in Austin—added a million dollars in their sales pipeline. Inside twelve months they had more than doubled their business revenue.

Why? Hard sells didn't work well on C-level execs making commercial real estate decisions. Experienced businesspeople—the "whales"—know how to fend off pushy salespeople (especially if they're young). By telling stories, the Colliers team shifted the conversation from yes/no to "story and takeaway." Executives were more apt to listen to a story about someone like them than to let a salesman stay on the line using high-pressure tactics. The team started closing larger sales because of more buy-in from higher-ups.

Thomas the introvert became the number one salesperson, outselling not just the extroverts but the company principals—the first-ever junior associate to do so! Switching to story-based selling worked so well that today, the entire team has a weekly thirty-minute meeting to share client stories with one another.

That's right; every week, the bulldog goes to "story time."

SIDESTEP OBJECTIONS

I discovered objection stories by accident. When I first started selling door-to-door, one of the objections I'd hear over and over again was, "Look, there's no way I'm going with Ozcom. I tried it and the coverage was terrible, so I switched back to Telstra."

It was true. When Ozcom first launched, it had nowhere near the coverage of the other major Australian telecom. I'd experienced it myself as a kid. How could I argue with a valid point that I knew to be true? I couldn't simply tell them, "You're wrong, we're great, sign here." I needed to find a way to handle their objection without invalidating their experience.

One day, the workaround fell in my lap: From out of nowhere, I got a call from a customer thanking me for convincing him to give Ozcom another try. The coverage had been fine, and he loved how much money he was saving—all the pieces of an objection story fell into place. The next time someone gave me the Ozcom versus Telstra coverage excuse, this is the story I gave them:

I perfectly understand and the last thing I want to do is waste any of your time. However, I just had a customer call me who had experienced the same bad coverage service, just like you.

When I was talking to him, he told me he wasn't interested in switching back from Telstra to Ozcom again. I was just about to walk out when I turned around and said to him, "When you first signed up with Ozcom, what did you do it for?"

He said, "To save money." Of course, I understand that. In a retail business with only a 20 percent margin, saving $1 is the same thing as selling $5.

I said to him, "So, originally you moved to save money but then had to move back because of the coverage, which makes sense. However, today, they've spent millions on new towers, and Ozcom now has 95 percent coverage while Telstra is 99 percent, so almost the same.

"Originally, you moved for savings and left for the coverage. So today, let's forget all that happened, and start with a new proposition. If you could have all the coverage and all the savings—wouldn't you jump at the chance?"

And he told me, "Well, what if it's not?"

I said, "You'll get a thirty-day, no-questions-asked, full money back guarantee."

Well, long story short, he called me just the other day to thank me, as he's now saving money and has all the coverage he needs.

So while I completely understand why it wasn't worth it for you to switch to Ozcom then, now with the coverage fixed—and of course I'll give you the same guarantee as him—isn't that like getting everything you wanted? Would you like to give it a try with a thirty-day safeguard to start saving $X?

I didn't tell him he was wrong. In fact, technically, I didn't even try to counter his objection; I sidestepped it altogether. I simply gave him a story about someone like him who had a similar objection but wound up being glad he made the decision to buy. People could pick apart my logical arguments, but they can't deny that this guy called and thanked me for getting him back to Ozcom.

I'm not asking them to accept or reject anything. I'm just sharing a story that appeals on an emotional level (the fear of loss, the thrill of savings). More important, they get to decide what the moral of the story is.

That's the beauty of stories. There's no right or wrong. There's nothing that's required from the listeners other than that they listen. It bypasses the automatic guards we put up, because a story doesn't ask you to consider facts; it doesn't need a response.

It just is.

DON'T SELL YOURSELF AS A SALESPERSON

Don't get me wrong; you are in sales.

If your livelihood depends on being able to persuade and influence others, then you are, first and foremost, a person who sells, regardless of whatever else you are. You have to embrace the fact that you sell for a living.

Alex has nothing to do if he doesn't generate projects to work on. Jim Comer can't speak without first landing the speaking gig. Zack can't coach clients without clients in the first place. You have to sell for everything else to happen. At the same time, however, you shouldn't think of yourself as a salesperson.

I tried a subtle mindset shift along these lines with Tommy, one of the first salespeople I trained when I became team manager at Ozcom. He came in about a month or so after I started my own company, and his sales were low and inconsistent. I taught him everything I used, but the first time he encountered an objection, the script flew out the window. Tommy came from a tough part of town and was used to quickly moving into "confrontation mode." Every time a sales call became the least bit argumentative, he immediately slipped into his old aggressive stance. Each talk became a fight that revolved around why the customer was wrong and why our product was better.

Finally, I pulled him aside and said, "Tommy, try this. Don't think of yourself as a salesperson. A salesperson is there to shove something down someone's throat. When you go in, before you talk to anybody, I want you to tell yourself, 'I'm not a salesman; I'm a sales consultant.' You're there to help them figure out what's best for them—not to sell them a telecom plan or die trying. Don't argue. Ask questions, like you would if you were their lawyer or accountant. Pretend you're a telecom expert, there to give your expert opinion."

It worked. He turned his focus from "winning" to "advising." If prospects objected, then it was either because Tommy didn't understand their situation or because they didn't understand how it would help them. Tommy went from telling them they were wrong to asking questions to find the gap between his "expert" opinion and their objections.

It also forced him to become a better listener. Instead of his previous strategy of tell, tell, tell, he started keying in on what they were actually saying. They didn't want to fight. They just wanted to make the best decision for them and their business. When he listened attentively, Tommy had a better context for overcoming objections. Instead of seeing it as a rejection, he eventually came to see it as misunderstanding. Either he misunderstood what was important to them, or they misunderstood how our providers solved the prospect's problem.

"Salesman" immediately brings to mind sleazy used car dealers and dodgy corporate types who care only about the size of their next commission check. That's not who and what you are. (If it is, you're reading the wrong book.)

If you're like me, you simply want to promote your products and services in a way that's authentic and congruent with who you are.

7

take their temperature
(STEP SIX: TRIAL CLOSE)

Never test the depth of the river with both feet.

—WARREN BUFFETT

Do you want to be a pushy salesperson?

Of course not. Even plenty of extroverts cringe when it comes to the hard sell. No one actually wants to do it. So why does the traditional approach to sales teach us to be aggressive?

It's to solve the same problem we all face when selling to people: their basic fear of loss. People would rather make no decision than make a bad one. They'd rather hang on to what they have than risk it in order to gain something better. It's where we get the saying, "A bird in the hand is worth two in the bush." It's safer to keep what they've got (i.e., their money) than to trade it for something better (i.e., a product or service that solves their problem).

One time while working as the state sales manager in South Australia, I was showing a rep how to sell in Adelaide. A married couple told me that before our meeting, they'd both agreed that they weren't going to sign anything that day. During the meeting, however, they got to a point where they both felt so comfortable that they just nodded at each other and moved forward on the sale. When you have your process polished to this degree, it's not just a sales meeting, it's a performance, much like a play.

Many salespeople believe they have to be pushy; they don't believe that there's any other way to get people to take action. They force people into making a decision, instead of sitting there patiently waiting, while the customer keeps thinking and thinking and thinking.

"Well, I'm not sure…"

"You know, let me talk to my wife about this…"

"I really need to consult with my pastor first…"

I've heard every excuse in the book from people who were afraid to make a decision. I've even done it myself, thinking, *You know, I bet I could find something better elsewhere,* or, *I don't really have time to do this right now, but maybe in a year…*

Don't worry. I'm not about to tell you that you have to be aggressive, or that you need to "ask for the sale." That's conventional thinking for pushy, extroverted salespeople. That's not who we are.

By the same token, if you give people all the time in the world, they'll take it. The more time you spend chasing a sale, the less time you have to chase other sales, much less attend to all the rest of your work. On another front, the more time you waste waiting for someone to make a decision, the less time you'll have for your other customers.

It's a catch-22. People need to be pushed, yet hate to be pushed; we need to push them, yet we hate to push. How can an introvert ask for the sale without outright asking for the sale?

How can we push without being pushy?

TOE IN THE WATER

I had asthma as a kid. I don't know if my parents were trying to help me or kill me, but they decided to sign me up for underwater swimming. (It turned out to benefit me by increasing my lung capacity, but I don't know if they knew that was going to happen.)

At the start of the season, you don't just jump in. The pool might still be freezing. You put a toe in the water to test the temperature. If it's warm enough, then you can dive in headfirst.

You see where I'm going with this. In fact, the idea is pretty standard in the conventional approach to sales. We're supposed to look for signs that people have warmed up to us—that they're ready to buy. Such signs include nodding their head, an open posture, a relaxed demeanor, and other such nonverbal cues. On the phone, we're supposed to listen to the tone of their voice, the words they use, and whether they're talking about the future (having already decided about the present).

Leave all that to the psychologists and fortune-tellers. Let me show you a far easier way to take someone's temperature. And my way doesn't require you to have years of experience studying micro-expressions and linguistics.

Have you ever said something that could be taken two ways—and the other person took it the wrong way? When you realize the miscommunication, you say, "Oh, no, I didn't mean it *that* way! What I meant was…"

"Playing it off" is when you really did mean it that way, but you see that doesn't sit well with your audience (or when you realize that you've potentially embarrassed yourself). So you play it off by acting as if you didn't mean it the way you actually meant it.

Let me show how to intentionally do this with sales.

Meshell Baker provides life coaching. When she's on a phone call with a potential client, after going through her questions and addressing their concerns and determining that they might be ready to make a decision, she'll ask the innocuous question, "So would you prefer to set up calls in the afternoons or in the evenings?"

If they say, "Yeah, you know, I think evenings would really work best for me," then it signals that they're already mentally moving forward with the coaching relationship. Unless and until they signal otherwise, Meshell assumes that they've already said yes—that she already has the sale.

She asked without asking.

However, if they say, "Hang on, Meshell, I'm not ready to make a decision just yet," she can easily play it off.

"Oh, no, I didn't assume you were. I just need to understand your preference so I can speak to how our sessions would work for you and your schedule."

That seemingly unimportant exchange actually accomplishes quite a lot. It:

1. Gives the prospect the nudge they need to make a decision.

2. Lets Meshell take the temperature to see if they've already made the decision in their mind without

putting pressure on them (or herself) by asking outright.

3. Puts the prospect in a slightly apologetic state of mind: "Oh, I'm sorry I misunderstood you, Meshell." That helps them feel like they owe her (even if it's just a little).

4. Lets Meshell know that she still has some work to do and more stories to tell.

If they don't pick an option, it means they're not ready to buy, which means that Meshell needs to go back to probing for pain points, translating features and benefits into stories. Instead of trying to force them to make a decision (the normal approach to sales), she can play it off, smoothly follow it up with another question, and go right back into Steps Three, Four, and Five.

When she finds what's holding them back from making a decision and they appear ready to pull the trigger, she can use a similar line for trial close, take two: "Now, I'm just looking at my schedule. Do Tuesday or Thursday evenings work better for you?" or, "Would you rather do these sessions in person or via Skype?"

THE DOUBLE-BIND

Even better, the tack I took with Meshell provides the additional benefit of introducing what we call a double-bind. You don't want to ask the customer, "Do you want this or not?"

It's a yes-or-no, black-or-white question. Plus, it's loaded with emotion: We don't want to be rejected, and the customer doesn't want the annoyance and/or guilt that comes with saying no.

Instead, Meshell's prospects face the question, "Do you want this one or that one?" That is, instead of yes or no, it makes them focus on option A or B. Here are just some of the double-bind trial closes I've used myself, with my sales teams or with my clients. Any of these nudge people down the path of taking action rather than deciding if they want to take action in the first place:

- ▶ "Now, did you prefer the black model or the silver?"
- ▶ "So, would a weekday or a weekend session work best for you?"
- ▶ "Would a day course or a night course suit you better?"
- ▶ "Okay, so would you prefer the self-guided online option or would you like to hear more about what working with me is like?"
- ▶ "So, does leasing or renting work best for you?"

Thanks to my strong marketing, I'm lucky enough to have people booked in to speak with me. These days, when speaking to a potential client, this is the trial close I use after going through questions and stories (where I give them real value to help them in whatever situation they're in): "Now, at this stage, I can do one of these three things. I can direct you to some great free content I created to help you create rapid growth for yourself..."

Let's stop and think about this for a second. Why do I offer free content? It taps into our basic instinct for reciprocity. In his book *Influence: The Psychology of Persuasion*, Robert Cialdini does a great job of showing how powerfully we feel the need to reciprocate, even when given something as seemingly inconsequential as a wildflower. By leading with the offer of something free, it makes me seem indifferent (i.e., in demand) and invokes the law of reciprocity: The prospects now feel like they are slightly in my debt. Also, having a free option helps get time-wasters out of your hair. If they want to jump right to the free option, then they really didn't want to pay in the first place.

Continuing on with my trial close, the next thing I say is, "Or I can talk to you about an academy I created where you can learn and work with a group of like-minded service providers, or I can talk to you about what working with me would look like. Do you have a preference?"

I don't ask them, "Which of these options do you want to buy?" Instead, I ask, "Which of these options do you want to pursue?"

They're telling me what they want me to sell them.

ask without asking

(STEP SEVEN: ASSUME THE SALE)

Optimism is the faith that leads to achievement. Nothing can be done without hope and confidence.

—HELEN KELLER

I once coached a man in Melbourne, Troy, who rented furniture to real estate companies staging unoccupied homes. People are more likely to buy if the living room has a sofa and a piece of art and when the bedroom has a bed and a dresser. People want to buy the vision they see, not an empty shell. They want to see it as a home, not just a house. This also helped with older estates with dated furniture that...well, smelled like old furniture. It's worth it to rent new furnishings for a few months to help sell the home more quickly and with less negotiating, just like employing the trick of baking fresh cookies. As we've said throughout this book, our desires aren't rational; we just find ways to rationalize what we want.

However, Troy had a problem with collecting payment from the homeowners. He billed them at the end of each month rented and as such, the homeowners had little incentive to pay him for the final month, after they'd already sold the house and he'd removed the furniture. Or even worse, they would contract the furniture for eight weeks and then want to keep the furniture for an extra week or two. They were fine with the extra fee...until it came time to pay. At that point, their phone seemed to go straight to voice mail. It got to the point that he was almost writing off the last month of each staging. It was just a headache.

I said, "Well, mate, why don't you just charge them a month up front? Bill them before you stage the house. That way, you collect at the beginning of the month. When you pick up the furniture, they're already paid up."

He said, "Nobody in our industry does that. No customer would use me if I charged them before I even delivered the furnishings."

"Really? When did you decide that?"

He just frowned. "I mean, I didn't *decide*...that's just how it's always been done."

"So, did someone tell you that? Or did you just assume that? And why would these sellers even know that? You told me that for almost all your customers, it's their first time staging a home like this."

I wasn't trying to be a smart aleck. I've just found that, so many times in life, we simply assume that things have to be a certain way. We spend our lives living by rules we've never tested. Who knows what can't be done until it's been tried? Even if "that's not how it's done" in your industry, does the customer know that? It's your business; you set the rules.

When I founded the Small Business Festival in Austin, people told me it took eight to twelve months to secure sponsorship for this kind of event, especially for the first time. And yet I locked in Capital One, GoDaddy, Facebook, the City of Austin, and WP Engine all within ninety days. When people tell me, "It's always been done like this," I just can't give it much weight.

Troy argued a bit until finally I said, "Look, do this for me: Just try it. Over the next two weeks, I want you to lead the price discussion with, 'So for us to put the furniture in, our standard process is to charge one month in advance. What is the easiest way for you to organize payment? Would it be by credit card or check?' If it's a card, say, 'Great—which one?' If it's by check, say, 'Perfect—can you go grab that for me, please?' Just try it and see what happens. In fact, why don't I go with you to your next sales call?"

The week after, we hopped in his car and drove to a prospective buyer's home. He introduced me as "someone who's training today" and then proceeded with his sales spiel. I chimed in here and there, but he did all the selling; I was just there to help with the payment arrangement.

I waited until I felt that the homeowner was excited about what he was hearing. Then I took his temperature by saying, "Excellent. So would it be easier for you to provide access to the property for staging on the weekend or during the week? The weekend? Fantastic."

That was the trial close. By indicating the time for us to start, he signaled that he's ready to buy. Once I saw that, I knew it was time to present the price.

"Now, industry wide, all furniture rentals are a month at a time"—per Troy—"plus a small staging cost, and for your home it would be $X per month with a $Y staging fee. Now, our standard process is one month in advance, and we need your driver's license number for security. Do you have a driver's license? Fantastic, would you grab that for me please?"

While the buyer was going for his wallet, I picked up the

paperwork and got on with writing out the contract. When he looked up, he saw me filling out paperwork, and we just moved forward.

"Okay, now, what's the easiest way to organize payment? Would that be credit card or check?"

As soon as he pulled out his checkbook, I said, "So that will be $2,500 for the first month and the staging fee." After I got the check, I suggested that using a credit card for the additional months might be easier, versus worrying about mailing checks. I joked that while we'd have to pay the credit fee, we'd be happy to eat those costs to make his life easier. He laughed and gave us his credit card details; we shook hands and left.

When we stepped outside the building, Troy turned to me and said, "That just happened, didn't it? He didn't even raise his eyebrows. He just acted like it was normal."

I said, "Mate, that's because we acted like it was normal. That was your 'standard process.' I didn't try to explain why we did it or really call attention to it at all. When he said he preferred weekend delivery, he'd already made the subconscious decision that he was buying. Everything else was just details. By the time I asked for payment, it was almost an afterthought.

"If he would've said, 'Now just a minute. I'm not ready to make a decision just yet,' I could have easily said, 'Oh, no, you misunderstood. I'm only asking, as we have to look at our crews' schedules to see their availability. I'm just getting all your information recorded to save time for later. See, we had a client just like you one time...' and gone straight into one of your clients' success stories."

As it was, we assumed the sale...and assumed rightly.

HOW TO HANDLE PRICE

"Look, I just need to know how much this is going to cost."

Ever take a phone call where that was the prospect's opening line? I've had emails asking straightaway how much I charge for business coaching. But you can't have an effective discussion on price until prospects understand your value.

That's why price comes last.

You have to get through establishing trust, asking questions, providing stories, and handling objections before you share how much you charge. With Troy's client, I didn't present price until I took his temperature and saw that he wanted what Troy was selling.

If your client asks about price or how much it is going to cost at any point before you're ready to discuss it—whether at the beginning of the meeting, while you're explaining the agenda, or at any time during your stories—all you have to say is, "[Name], we'll certainly get to that, but at this stage I'm still going through the process of understanding exactly what will work for you and tailoring a solution that will fit your needs perfectly. We will get to price in a second, I promise, but is it okay if I ask you a few more questions first? Excellent." And back to your script.

Alternatively, you might say, "Is it okay if I finish explaining how this product/service worked for [past client] so I can confirm that what I'm suggesting 100 percent fits what you're looking to achieve? Excellent." And back to your script.

As I said back in Chapter 2, when delivering your agenda, make sure to include when price will be discussed. By doing so, just like I showed you in the Pollard Institute example, potential customers will feel confident that you know what you're doing and will be far less likely to jump the gun.

Why put off price until the very last?

If you lead with price, then every feature or benefit (individually) you present will automatically be gauged against that price: *Is that worth what they're quoting? I don't think so.* Now you have forced yourself into the position of wrestling with prospects' logical mind instead of appealing to their emotions.

If price comes last, you get the benefit of the compounding effect. If you mention price too soon, you are relying on one specific feature or benefit to tip the scales, as opposed to allowing them to build on each other to the point that, when price is mentioned, the prospect's line of thought becomes, *I can get all of this for that? Sounds like an amazing deal!*

If you quote before knowing exactly what prospects need, then you're chasing a moving target. Suppose they need something that costs more than your standard price or what you had anticipated. You'd need to increase your quoted price. However, they would feel cheated: You said it would cost X, but now you're saying Y.

There really is no win for you mentioning price sooner.

Now, let's address the elephant in the room. We all know price is a big deal, right? Wrong! Price is a big deal only if you make it one. You just finished reading the story of how I discussed price in Troy's example. Notice how little time I spent on it. It was almost as if I were just talking about what color the moving trucks were, an almost inconsequential fact. The words I used also came across as somewhat indifferent.

If you give price more attention than it deserves, you will come across like it's a lot of money. Your tone and demeanor might make them think, *Hmm, maybe I should think about this before jumping in...*

Present your price just as if you were talking about anything else. Of course, I know it's nearly impossible to feel indifferent about price. As a matter of fact, in talking about this book and how to address pricing, someone told me that I could write a whole chapter—heck, a whole book!—just on pricing and how to present it.

I could—but it's really not that big of a deal. Your price is the price. Say it and move on.

If you can't get past the idea that you're asking for a lot of money, you have to desensitize yourself to the number. For example, a good friend of mine owned a karate studio in a low- to middle-class neighborhood. He hired local high school kids to go door-to-door selling a yearlong program that cost $3,500.

Think back to your time in high school. I don't care when you graduated, $3,500 is a lot of money. For these kids, it was no different. They did amazingly well pitching the parents on the program, its value, and the structure. When it came to price, though, they almost stuttered as it came out of their mouths. He realized that the kids were terrified of saying a number that big.

He set out on a mission to desensitize them to it. Before the start of business, he'd get the kids to practice saying to each other "thirty-five hundred." Not "three thousand, five hundred" but "thirty-five hundred."

- ▶ "That's thirty-five hundred pillows..."
- ▶ "That's thirty-five hundred feathers..."
- ▶ "That's thirty-five hundred giraffes..."

They just practiced and practiced until the price meant nothing to them; it was just a number. It took about a week of this routine, but he saw an amazing difference: The price tag of "thirty-five hundred dollars" just rolled off their tongues, and sales skyrocketed.

- ▶ If you charge $15,000, get practicing. "That's fifteen K. That's fifteen K. That's fifteen K."
- ▶ If you have a payment plan, practice that too: "That's twelve-and-a-half K—seventy-five hundred llamas up front, and two simple monthly payments of twenty-five hundred llamas."
- ▶ If you charge $8,400: "It's eighty-four hundred monkeys—that's four equal payments of twenty-one hundred monkeys."

Keep going until your price means nothing.

DON'T TREAT SALES LIKE GLASS

The "greats"—Zig Ziglar, Brian Tracy, and others—live by the idea that you must be persistent. "It takes seven noes to get a yes," and other quotes like that tell us that we are supposed to keep asking, keep pursuing, and keep badgering our customers until they finally give in.

Well, a thick-skinned extrovert may have no trouble hounding someone until they finally relent, but for most of us introverts, that's just not congruent with who we are.

In selling door-to-door for Ozcom, I couldn't afford to revisit a store five or six times just to make a twenty-dollar commission. Between petrol and parking meters, I would barely break even.

Even when I started my own telecom brokerage, sales commissions were only a couple of hundred dollars. If our salespeople made four or five appointments a day, and it took five appointments to make a sale, and assuming they had an astounding ratio of closing one in every two customers, that would be five hundred dollars a week—at the very best.

I had one sales guy named Grant who did an amazing job at developing rapport. Customers loved him. But he never closed a sale on the first meeting. Never. He'd go back again, then again, and then again. When he finally did close, some of his deals were huge, but it took forever to get there.

I said, "Grant, why aren't you closing more quickly? Obviously, you can sell these big orders. Why does it take you five appointments to sell $1,000 worth of commission?"

He said, "Matt, the way I see it, if I sell an average of $1,000 over five meetings, I make $200 each meeting. It's the same amount of money, and I don't have to feel pushy."

"But wouldn't you rather sell $1,000 in one go? And then instead of going back another four times, sell $1,000 each to other customers? Wouldn't you rather use five visits to make $1,000 each than one at $200?"

Obviously, yes, but he couldn't get past his mental image of being the pushy salesman, as well as his fear of losing the sale if he were perceived as one. He treated each potential sale like glass: If he wasn't careful, he'd break it.

The thing was, he didn't need to be pushy. I'd developed the sales script specifically for introverts like him and me. In the script, he was supposed to say, "Okay, now I need to ensure that you qualify for this. Do you have an ABN? Fantastic, would you like to go grab that for me? Excellent."

Rarely did anyone ever have that on-hand, so they'd have to get out of their chair, walk down to someone else's office, get the number, and come back. Often, just this little nudge to action is all they needed to help them make the decision. When they returned, I (or whoever was running the script) would be filling out the paperwork to get things rolling.

This is the social equivalent of Newton's First Law of Motion: An object either remains at rest or in motion until acted upon by an outside force. The very act of the person getting out of the chair puts the sale in motion. Once things are in motion, it's easier to let them stay in motion than to dig your heels in and call a stop to it.

It worked. Everyone in my brokerage company used it (by mandate; if you worked on my sales team, you memorized the script I'd worked out that I knew worked and delivered consistent results, regardless of the person or personality). So why was Grant having such a hard time?

When it came time to ask for the ABN...he just stopped. When I asked him why he felt he was being pushy, he said, "It's just—I worry about losing the sale. I feel disingenuous about asking for their ABN, and I think they can see that."

"Okay, Grant, here's what we're going to do. First, you're going to treat sales like rocks, not glass. They're not going to break. Second, because you spend so much time with each customer, you have only a few in your pipeline at any one time. You're afraid of losing even one of them because it represents a big part of your potential commissions. Third, here's a new rule: If the customer doesn't sign up, you can't go back *and* you get only one more meeting with all your current prospects."

He said, "What? What do you mean?"

"If they don't sign up that day, you can't go back. I don't care if they call back the next day and say they've changed their mind and want to buy everything you sell—you can't go back."

Grant said, "That's gonna cost me money, Matt. I can't do that."

Let's stop for a moment and talk about one of the most fundamental things you have to keep in mind as you learn how to use all of this: You have to be willing to risk things getting worse before you do better. You may not be getting great results doing things the way you do them now, but at least you feel comfortable doing them that way and at least you're getting them consistently, right?

When you start changing things up, you won't know what you're doing. It will feel uncomfortable. Just like moving from an automatic car to a manual. Eventually you will have greater control, but for a while it will be a bit jerky. Learning to ski felt unnatural (standing on two sticks that want to point in different directions, throwing yourself down a slope...just writing this, it sounds crazy), but I enjoyed it once I learned how to do it. You can't get better until you change something.

I said, "Grant, you have to trust me. This is going to get you paid, not the other way around. I mean, these customers like you, but eventually they need to buy or go with someone else. And, well, let's face it: They are at work to work, not hang out with you.

"Look, let's just do this as a one-week experiment. Are you willing to try this just for one week, with the potential outcome being that you sell as much as the other guys and potentially much, much more?"

He nodded.

"It's not necessarily about being more pushy, Grant. I don't know what's going to be different for you. You may become indifferent, feeling that you're not going to get the sale, because most people don't sign up with you on the first meeting anyway. That lack of desperation may help the prospect feel like you're more relaxed.

"On the other hand, knowing that you have only one shot to get it right, you may do a more thorough job of figuring out what the customers really need and translating features to benefits for them. I don't know. But I do know this: If you have to push to make it happen, you're doing it wrong."

We practiced the sales team's script until he'd nailed the "I need to ensure that you qualify" part. He went out and closed almost every one of his new sales calls with just one meeting. Then he called his big prospects back and asked if he could go through everything with them again. He treated each one like it was a new sale. Bam!—a $10,000 commission deal! Grant made more money that month than any other rep and kept that winning streak for six months straight.

In a sales team that relies on a system like mine, if one person is over-performing, you need to figure out what they're doing and replicate it. If they're under-performing, like Grant, you want to figure out what's wrong and fix it.

That one change took him from the bottom of the heap to the top. It didn't matter if he was selling to the owner of a small shop with one mobile plan or pitching a complex sale to a CEO with twenty or thirty mobile plans. He'd still organize the entire deal, from meeting to signing, in one day.

(This isn't unique to Grant. I have clients who sell $10,000 courses and $25,000 products in one call. The record for the cadre of self-employed service professionals I coach currently stands at selling $75,000 from an unplanned, in-bound thirty-minute phone call from someone the service rep had never met before. And he's done it more than once.)

FIND A WAY, NOT AN EXCUSE

I'm not suggesting that you never follow up with a prospect. You don't necessarily have to institute the rule for yourself that I did with Grant (though the experiment obviously propelled him to success). However, I do need you to realize that selling five figures' worth of products and services from a single phone call is not only possible but normal—and that if you don't do it in your first meeting, someone else may come behind you and do it before your next chance.

You can't use the excuse that your industry or product or market is different. I sold a five-figure sponsorship for Small Business Festival to Capital One in just one meeting. I had another meeting where I sold over one hundred people into a nationally accredited training program. Sure, there was a lot of paperwork, but we went from "Who is this guy?" to "Yes, we'll put all of our teams through the course" in just one sitting.

Speaking of paperwork, don't let it be an excuse, either. In one telecom sale, I happened to walk into a gas station where the owner kept his office...for all forty of his other gas stations. I sold him telecom plans for all of them. He said, "Okay, well, fill out all the paperwork and bring it back."

My response: "Do you have a table? I can do them all right now."

He was surprised for a moment, but said, "You can use a cafeteria table, I guess."

"Perfect!"

I sat at the gas station dining booth for three hours filling out the paperwork for all forty locations. Once I was done, I marched into his office, we laughed about it, and I signed one of my biggest deals ever at Ozcom. If I had left, he could have changed his mind, but after seeing me work so hard filling out all his paperwork...what was he going to do but say, "Let's do this!"

You may not have found a way to seal the deal in one meeting, but that doesn't mean it doesn't exist. Again, the beauty is that you don't have to push harder. You don't have to be aggressive. You don't need to be anything other than you. You just need to experiment until you find a way that feels natural for you. Trust in the process, assume the sale, and they will come.

But what do you do when they don't?

perfect the process

> The competitor to be feared is one who never bothers about you at all, but goes on making his own business better all the time.
>
> **—HENRY FORD**

Plenty of people believe that Henry Ford invented the automobile. He didn't, of course. It had been around for almost two decades by the time he founded Ford Motor Company. His genius was in his assembly line.

But he didn't invent the assembly line, either. Breaking down a product into its component parts and having a person specialize in creating that one piece (instead of building the whole thing, like a blacksmith or a carpenter would have in medieval times) was what launched the Industrial Revolution in England.

In fact, some historians point to the Venetian Arsenal as possibly the first industrial-scale "assembly line," creating an entire warship in just a day...in Venice of 1104. For those of you at home, that's one year shy of eight *centuries* before the first Model T rolled out the door.

So why, then, is Henry Ford regarded as one of the greatest businesspeople and industrialists ever? How did he beat out dozens, perhaps even hundreds, of other automobile manufacturers to become the titan he was? How is he to this day still among the top ten richest people who ever lived in modern history?

His secret? He never stopped improving his process.

He constantly tinkered with every facet of his manufacturing operations, trying to wring just an extra thirty seconds out of this or an extra two minutes out of that. Everything he did was designed for efficiency—then disassembled and reassembled for even more. He had every moment and even every movement down to an exact science.

In fact, as a rep from Castrol, my dad worked in a Ford plant. Even in the early 2000s, Ford went through the effort of training assembly line workers to pull the exact number of bolts out of a bucket that they'd need for each task. That way, they wouldn't waste precious seconds reaching back into the bin.

If most salespeople were to manufacture cars the way they approach sales, they'd say, "Look, we're just gonna put all these machines in a room—just wherever they'll fit—and we'll just figure it out for each car as we go along."

They go into a meeting, pick up the phone, or go to a networking event and figure they'll just wing it. They may have even assembled a hodgepodge process that works for them and produces just enough results to keep them limping along. In that case, their attitude is "This is the best I can do, and if it's not broke, don't fix it."

If Ford had had that attitude, we probably wouldn't even know his name. He'd be a footnote in the annals of the automobile industry. But because of his focus—some might almost say obsession—with process and efficiency, he kept getting incrementally better.

With some changes, you may jump ahead by miles instead of inches. For me, the big leap was seeing the sales process for what it is: a big assembly line. Learning how to use stories to sell, how to turn features into tangible benefits, asking the right questions, figuring out the assumptive sell—those lessons propelled me past all the other salespeople to become the number one salesperson in the entire company. That's how I started closing one in every fifty sales calls, then one in every twenty, then one in ten, then one in five. Figuring out which questions were more effective or how to best tell one particular story—and, especially, the moral of how this product is awesome and will fix their problem—allowed me to incrementally improve how I could close one in four, then one in three... and sometimes even nine in ten.

I can't claim credit for any of the building blocks I've presented in this book. As I said, I pieced them together from YouTube videos when I was eighteen years old. You can go out and find plenty of sales books on each aspect. I didn't invent the idea of continuous improvement. I've just figured out that it works in introverts' sales, too.

If you read this book and use it to get more customers, great. It will have been worth your time. But if you stop once you get out of the hole you're in, then you've tapped into only a fraction of the benefit. You don't just want to learn to sell—you want to learn how to keep getting better.

DO AN EVAL ON YOURSELF. REALLY.

Your sales system should constantly evolve, constantly improve, and constantly be the center of your business's attention. The day you neglect your sales system is the day you start sliding back to where you started.

The first step to improving your process: Make sure to actually use the process. When my sales guys started seeing a dip in their sales, my first question was: "Did you stick to the script?"

"Oh, yeah, absolutely!"

"Great! Role-play with me."

They would immediately give me this *Oh, crap!* look. They'd do it. Inevitably, some parts were out of order, some were skipped, some were summarized.

I'd say, "Okay, go home and read it tonight. That's exactly what you say to your customers tomorrow."

They'd go back to the exact wording on the script and their sales would pick right back up to normal. Circumstances hadn't changed; they were just running a suboptimal version of the system.

You need to do something similar. Every time you get off the phone, get back to your car, or go back behind the counter, stop and evaluate the sales experience. Don't wait until the end of the day or the end of the week. The longer you take to review the sale, the more details you'll miss and forget. Do an analysis while the incident is still fresh in your mind.

First, don't make excuses about why you didn't make the sale:

- "They weren't going to buy anyway."
- "They'd already made up their mind before I opened my mouth."
- "They weren't my ideal customer."
- "They were probably more trouble than they were worth."
- "I was just off my game today."
- "It's just that time of the year."
- "People just don't buy when it's raining."
- "They probably couldn't afford it."
- My personal favorite: "It was just an unlucky day."

The specific excuse you use may be true, and you're not ever going to win 100 percent of sales, but you can always improve your odds of success. The better your sales system, the less those other factors matter.

However, blaming those external factors will never help you get better. When you do that, you give up control. You're saying that you couldn't have done anything to affect the outcome, that the results were destined to happen. You subconsciously admit that you're powerless to change things.

On the other hand, I don't want you to obsess over a sale, either. You shouldn't beat yourself up and feel that you're a terrible salesperson. Neither of these extremes helps you objectively evaluate the sale.

Instead, ask yourself:

1. Did I stick to the script?
2. What could I have possibly done better?

3. What should I change?

Let each sale you miss clue you in on what you could do better.

ONE THING AT A TIME

In a true scientific experiment, the scientists—be they chemists, psychologists, statisticians, or whoever—alter only one variable at a time. Otherwise, they can never be sure which change produced the results they saw. If your doctor gave you five different treatments, how would you know which one cured you? If you started taking five different medications and developed an allergy, how would you know which one caused it?

When you begin succeeding at sales, you'll probably begin to get excited. You'll begin to see all the things you could be doing differently or better. You'll be tempted to make all kinds of changes. But you can never measure yourself or your process's improvement if you don't have a baseline and if you change more than one variable at a time.

When you first put your sales process together, everything is new. As you move forward, most of your changes should be major ones: introducing stories to sidestep objections or figuring out how to establish credibility.

As you progress and your process becomes more and more reliable, most of your changes will become more minor: the way you phrase a new question to uncover a pain point or how you introduce a particular story. When things don't work, go back to your basic process, reestablish your baseline, and then keep on moving forward toward perfection.

10

the introvert's edge in real life

Pay no attention to the man behind the curtain.

—THE WIZARD OF OZ

Despite my Irlen Syndrome, I'm proud to say that I've become an award-winning blogger. The time it takes me to write a great fifteen-hundred-word post, though, is huge as well as agonizing.

I knew that I wanted to share my sales system for introverts with a bigger audience. That meant writing a book. The thought, however, of writing tens of thousands of words, of going back and forth editing, and going through a manuscript time and time again plagued me for years.

That is, until the solution called me out of the blue.

I could share with you how that came to be, but honestly, since Derek's already ghostwriting this, I think I'll just let him tell it.

THE GHOST OF BUSINESS PAST

It's weird to come out from behind the curtain.

Then again, it'd be weird to ghostwrite about myself from Matthew's point of view.

Putting the stories of his other clients down on paper is easy because I don't have an emotional connection to them. They're just stories about people I've never met or met only in passing.

When it comes to my own story, though, it's a battle to keep emotion at bay. Even as I put this story to paper, I have tears welling up, threatening to spill over.

Let me paint a picture for you of where I was the moment before I picked up the phone to call Matthew: depressed, scared, and at my wits' end. I hadn't landed a new ghostwriting client in over a year, and I'd already finished my other projects. What little money I had saved was rapidly dwindling, and there were no prospects on the horizon.

Things were bleak, to say the least.

For much of my married life, my wife had been the primary breadwinner while I went to grad school and then again after I quit my job (with her encouragement) to work for myself.

It took some time, but I found a measure of success. In fact, I'm proud to have been the sole income earner while she went to grad school herself, went through her clinical training, and then during her maternity leave with our second child. Thank God she went back to work when she did, though, because that's just about when the bottom fell out of my business.

I went for over a year without landing a new client. Fortunately, one of my authors had opted to stretch her project out over a year, but after it concluded, I was staring at a shrinking bank account and growing credit card debt, with no prospects in the pipeline. That, plus tens of thousands of dollars in healthcare bills from my wife's difficult pregnancy and childbirth (combined with crappy insurance through her grad school) made me one scared son of a gun.

I'd proved to myself that I could do it. I'd been the sole provider for our family for a year and a half. Why couldn't I land any more clients? What was I doing wrong? Was this a sign from God? Had it been a run of good luck, but was it now time to return to the world of men and get a real job? Were my dreams crashing down around me?

During a monthly mastermind group that I hosted with a select group of other ghostwriters—when admittedly I felt like a fraud—my colleagues all offered ideas to help. One suggested I find a business coach and offer to trade services: ghostwriting for coaching. That very day, I happened to see a LinkedIn article that someone shared about niche marketing.

I thought, *It doesn't get much more niche than business ghostwriting,* so I followed the link and read the article. It made intuitive sense to me; I thought the author was really on to something. I followed his bio and landed on a website that was little more than a "coming soon" page. I found the contact page and fired off an email, figuring that the guy would probably blow me off.

About twenty minutes later, the phone rang.

After a brief sketch of the problem, Matthew somehow magically pinpointed exactly where I was in my business, exactly what my problem was, and exactly what I'd been trying to do to fix it. In fact, his accuracy was a little unsettling.

From that, I knew this guy could help me. I also knew there was no way in hell I could afford him. I tentatively pitched him the idea of trading coaching for writing.

He laughed and said, "I was just getting ready to look for a writer to help with an ebook I'm doing with a colleague." Though we were both a little wary (and each could tell that about the other), we agreed to work together on an ad hoc basis.

I'm not sure I ever told Matthew before writing this, but the only reason I agreed (even though I'd been the one to suggest it) was because I had nothing to lose and was grasping at straws. I didn't like "sales and marketing guys" because I always found them full of themselves, all bluster and bullshit and little else. I also detested the fact that Matthew subscribed to neurolinguistic programming. I thought it was pseudoscience and, at its core, manipulative. Last but not least, I hated trading services. I'm a free-market capitalist: If you want to trade for services, go find a commune. Like my power company, I take only cash.

I put on my happy face and went into the kitchen to tell my wife about my new arrangement. Years later, she confessed that she, too, thought I was grasping at straws. But I'd literally tried everything else I could think of, from going back to copywriting to redesigning my website to even trying to find employment. Nothing had worked. We were at the point where, if something didn't break, I'd have to swallow my pride and go beg my old boss for my job back.

Over the next couple of weeks, Matthew coached me while I worked on the ebook. My biggest revelation was that I didn't do sales. I just didn't. I liked marketing and, consequently, I was a decent marketer. Sales was a whole different story. I'm an introvert. (I mean, I'm a self-employed service professional who writes books all day and works with only a handful of people a year. I am the poster child for professional introverts.) My basic approach was to let my marketing do all the heavy lifting so that the sale would happen naturally.

When Matthew started talking about a sales script, I instinctively shied away. I didn't want to sound like a robotic telemarketer following a rote script. But then again, my way hadn't been working so well.

I soon had a sales call. I didn't really feel confident about going through the process Matthew had helped me create (*The Introvert's Edge* lite, you could call it), but I went through each step as I was supposed to. In thirty minutes, the client was ready to sign.

I hung up the phone and sat there, stunned. *Did that just happen? Did I just land a book in thirty minutes? For real?*

Over the next two-and-a-half weeks, I sold $80,000 worth of ghostwriting and editing work. By the end of six months, I'd sold more than I had in the previous three years *combined.*

I could take you through the following three years, but let me give you the CliffsNotes version:

- ▶ We went from financially struggling to debt-free and financially affluent.
- ▶ We moved from a (cute) little starter home in an older neighborhood with my office in the garage to a gorgeous home that we still have trouble believing is ours.
- ▶ My children have trust funds for their education. Regardless of scholarships, awards, or anything, when they each turn eighteen, we'll have enough to write a check for their bachelor's degrees from nearly any public university.

▶ I now have retirement investments, and we've set up another one for my wife aside from her employer's plan. If we do nothing but continue to invest the quite manageable amount we're contributing right now, we'll not only retire as millionaires but be able to live comfortably on the interest and pass the principal on to our children and grandchildren.

▶ I traveled to Zurich on business.

▶ I took my wife to London and Paris.

▶ As of the weekend before we submitted this book to the publisher, I closed a ghostwriting deal big enough that I don't need another client for another year.

If you would have told me the moment before I took Matthew's call that this would be my life in the next three years, I'd have asked you to share whatever you'd been smoking. It had to be some good stuff.

Honestly? It took me at least two years before I finally accepted that this was normal. I'd lived in fear for so long that I didn't know any other way to feel. I kept waiting for someone to drive up to my house and say, "Derek, look, this has all been a social experiment. You enjoyed it, but the study's over. Time to get back to reality. You've got twenty-four hours to move your stuff out."

Hasn't happened yet.

All this because Matthew showed me how to leverage my strengths as an introvert, to stop shying away from sales, and to put together a basic sales process that worked for me—

something that fit the way I did business, not that forced me to go against my nature.

Today, I step outside and the sky looks different. The air smells different. I see my life and my world as having changed. But nothing around me has changed; I have.

WHAT I DID THEN

What did I actually do to sell $80,000 in under three weeks?

I've tried every kind of outbound marketing: cold-calling, cold email, direct mail, LinkedIn networking, in-person networking, etc., etc., etc. I've never been able to make it work for landing ghostwriting gigs. Every dollar I've ever made came from people finding me, primarily through finding my website.

Before Matthew's coaching, when I got an email, I would have tried to do as much preselling in my response as possible. I'd send an email back chock-full of information with five or seven attachments of even more information. I wanted my potential authors to make up their mind by reading all of it and then simply pick up the phone once they'd made a decision. As Matthew pointed out, no one wants to entrust their book—perhaps the summary of their life's work—to someone based on an email and some PDFs. I wrote those long emails because they're what I wanted to send, not what potential authors wanted to see.

This time, I simply responded with a short, gracious note and a few suggested times for a phone call. We confirmed the times, and I did nothing else.

When we got on the phone, I walked through the main steps of my freshly minted sales process:

Rapport: I asked where the two would-be coauthors lived, and then we talked (which turned into joking) about our respective accents (Southern, British, and Australian).

Questions: I asked about the book they had in mind and asked a few clarifying questions to show that I understood what they wanted.

Stories: I told them two stories. The first was about three authors I'd worked with who needed help figuring out what they even wanted to write about and how the process of working with me resulted in a restructuring of their entire business process. The second story involved a French-German consultant whose husband, upon reading the ghostwritten manuscript, looked up from the couch and said, "Wow—this sounds just like you."

That was it. Notice that I didn't have an agenda, qualification process, or objection-handling cushions—there were plenty of things I had yet to embrace in Matthew's approach. Yet even with those things missing, and just using this bare-bones process, I still nailed $80,000 in sales.

After a little more conversation, I didn't even have to ask for the sale. They asked what my fee was. I told them. They thought it sounded good and asked me to send over the papers.

I went through the same process twice in the next week with another ghostwriting project and then a smaller editing project. Over three phone calls totaling about three hours, I'd changed the course of my life—personally and professionally.

WHAT I DO NOW

I still don't consider myself a great salesperson. Just decent.

But that's all I've needed to gross a healthy six-figure income every year. My sales process has gotten a little more sophisticated, and my bank account reflects that. The better I get, the more I sell. Sometimes I think, *Man, I'm getting pretty good at this sales stuff!*

At one point, though, my confidence led to overconfidence. I started to see my sales slump. In fact, I was in a sales lull for about six months. Those awful feelings of desperation started seeping back into my bones. My fears I thought conquered came back to haunt me.

I reached back out to the man who'd saved me before.

Matthew's first question: "Well, are you following your script?"

I said, "Well...it's kind of grown organically..."

We went back over it and I saw where I'd let some things slip. Two weeks later, I closed a deal that took me to the Swiss Alps; a month after that, another one took me to London.

I went back to the basics and things picked right back up.

I'll show you what I do now, but keep in mind that by the time this book goes to press, I will have tweaked something. In fact, working on this chapter with Matthew gave me a chance to get even more coaching on my sales script. I will incorporate those changes and do some modifications of my own. They might work, they might bomb, or they might be inconsequential, but I will experiment with something—the key being: one thing at a time.

My sales leads continue to come from online sources, primarily via either organic searches (just a straightforward Google search) or a keyword search that triggers a pay-per-click ad (PPC). Many of my marketing efforts focus on search engine optimization (SEO), but I've also published a book (*The Business Book Bible*), been a guest on a few podcasts, and done a smattering of other things to help people find me.

But—and let me make this clear so as to underscore the point of this book—I'm not trying to just get more traffic, or even just more quality traffic. I didn't need a book or PPC to sell that ice-breaking $80,000. In fact, without a decent sales process, all those tools would have gotten me is more inquiries, not more sales. I didn't do anything different but *learn how to sell to people already in front of me.*

I'm about to show you how 80 percent of my calls go.

Honestly? Seeing my sales script laid out in black and white for all the world (or at least the people who read this book) to see makes me uneasy. I worry that you'll feel that I'm disingenuous by having such a routine down. But it's worth it if it helps introverts like me find success pursuing their dreams, too.

I've found that in a phone call, being prepared and in control helps me be my authentic self; instead of having to mull over a question or comment, I can be in the moment. I can focus more on the client's response instead of having to come up with my own. Before I had a sales process, I didn't have any preparation for a phone call at all. I tried to do all my selling through email. The client would, by default, lead the conversation. The discussion on price would happen far too early, well before the author had a chance to appreciate what I brought to the table. I'd respond as best I could, but inevitably I'd get off the call feeling like I'd somehow failed. In times of self-denial, I'd blame the authors for why they wouldn't choose me as their ghostwriter: They couldn't afford me, they didn't know what they wanted, they feared I didn't have the requisite experience, or any of a dozen other reasons why my failure at sales was their fault.

None of the above were true. Once I had a basic sales process in place, all of a sudden money wasn't an issue, they knew exactly what they wanted, and they were impressed with the level of experience I'd had with other authors just like them.

Knowing how the call is going to go takes the worry off what I should say and how I should respond. I already have the hard part out of the way. Instead of worrying about my performance, I can let that automatic stuff happen almost without conscious effort. That frees me up to be fully present: to concentrate on what they're saying instead of stressing to figure out how I should respond when they finish speaking.

This is how upward of 80 percent of my sales calls go:

Step 1: Trust and agenda.

(Get on conference line.)

"Hi, this is Derek."

(Wait for response.)

"[Name], it's nice to meet you, thank you for reaching out. Now, where are you?"

(Wait for response, then short chat or benign joke about location.)

"Well, this is how I usually suggest these calls go. I'll let you tell me about your professional background, from when you started your career to where that's brought you to today. Then I'll give you a quick snapshot of the kinds of authors I work with and the types of projects I collaborate on. Then, you'll tell me about your idea for your book and where you are with it. Then I'll quickly walk you through the five-step process I use for every project. Then we can talk about the different service packages I offer and my fee for each. Does that sound good?"

(Wait for response.)

"Great. Okay, I'll give you the floor. Tell me about [full name]."

(Intently listen to their professional background. Laugh or comment appropriately.)

"*Thanks for sharing all of that. It gives me a good idea of where you're coming from. To give you a quick snapshot of myself, I work almost exclusively with business thought leaders like you. I've worked with authors on five continents, including a Turkish economist, a Texas oil tycoon, an IT start-up millionaire, a Brazilian federal judge, and a Cajun colonel.*

"*My authors work with the International Monetary Fund, DaimlerChrysler, SAP, Disney, the Marine Corps, and even the Red Cross. After a few years of working with these types of authors, I got frustrated that there wasn't a good resource I could turn to on how to write these types of books, so I actually wrote the book on how to write thought leadership books,* The Business Book Bible, *which came out a few years ago.*

"*My typical author has been in business for ten to twenty years and has run their own company for at least five to ten. Now, of course, everybody wants their book to be a bestseller; however, for my authors, commercial success is a secondary goal. They write their book primarily to be a platform book: something to help them market their expertise, help them secure speaking gigs, or promote their other products or services.*

"*So all of that is to say: You are exactly the kind of author I work with. If you had come to me saying, 'Derek, I'd like to write a memoir or vampire erotica,' I'd say, 'Sorry—that's not my bag.' But business thought leadership? That's what I do all day, every day.*"

If they spoke only to their professional background ear-lier: "Now, tell me about your book."

If they started talking about their background and then wandered into talking about their book idea, say, "So, we've already started talking about your book, but—" and move on to Step 2.

Step 2: Ask probing questions.

Ask selected questions, based on information and/or concerns raised in their spiel.

(Because of Matthew's coaching in not only my sales but my marketing, my authors' concerns are so similar that I indirectly address them throughout the sales call. I don't have to ask too many probing questions because al-most all of their pain points are identical.)

"Let me ask you this: Fast-forward to one year from now. We've already finished your manuscript, we've gone through what it takes to turn it into a real book, and you're holding it in your hands. What do you do with your book?"

"How long have you been thinking about writing your book? A year? Two years? Ten?"

"Have you decided whether you want to go the tradi-tional publishing route or the self-publishing route?"

Step 3: Qualification.

"Now, do you have a business partner or coauthor, or are you going to be writing this book by yourself?"

(If not sole author): "Okay, great. I've worked on plenty of multiauthor projects. It adds a layer of complexity but nothing to worry about. When should we set up a call with them to talk about their involvement with the book?"

(If sole author): "Okay, great. Now, what about approval? Do you have investors or others who'll be involved in final approval of the book, or do we even need to worry about that?"

Step 4: Story-based selling.

"You know, I've never had an author who came to me who knew exactly what their book was about, exactly how they wanted it laid out, exactly what Chapter 1 was about, exactly what Chapter 2 was about—most of the time, they just know that they want to write a book. My authors don't come to me because they need someone who knows how to put a sentence together; they come to me because they need someone who can help them get all of their years of ideas and experiences out of their head and onto paper in a way that people actually want to read. So, you're in good company."

(Wait for response.)

"Now, it took me a little while to figure that out. I've changed the way I work with my authors over the years to accommodate this stage of figuring out what the book's about in the first place.

"Let me tell you about the five-step process I use to get it

out of your head and into a manuscript. I'm going to quickly list them, and then go through each one.

"There's discovery, blueprint, Frankendraft, edit, and polish.

"The discovery process starts off with me flying to your city for a three-day author retreat where we lock ourselves in a hotel suite or office and we do a brain purge. You'll tell me everything you've done over the last ten or twenty years: your ideas, your experiences, your stories, your expertise—anything and everything you feel might be even remotely related to the book. I'll record all of it and send it to my transcriptionist in Kansas. Then we schedule two weeks of follow-up calls to go over anything else you might have remembered. At the end of all of it, we'll have this mountain of raw material to use as we move forward in figuring out what your book's about.

"In step two, we create a blueprint. I sort and sift through these hours and hours of conversations to find the underlying themes in your book. We'll work together to say, 'This is the book's One Reader, this is their problem, and this is how the book solves it. This is what goes in Chapter 1: content, stories, examples, quotes, and whatever else. This is what goes in Chapter 2, Chapter 3.' So we have this working outline of what we're doing with the book.

"In step three, I ghostwrite the first chapter, send it to you, you read it, we get on the phone, and you tell me what you like, what you don't like, what sounds like you, what doesn't, any new ideas you've had, and what we should do

going forward. I take all of that information and ghost-write the second chapter. I send it to you, you read it, and we go through the whole process again. Chapter by chapter, we're gaining clarity on your vision for your book. We're shaping it even as we're creating it.

"At the end of that, we have our Frankendraft. I call it that because writing a book is less about painting the Mona Lisa and more about bringing life to a Frankenstein monster that's pieced and stitched together from dozens of different parts. It's not pretty—but it's alive.

"In step four, I go back to the beginning and rewrite the entire manuscript based on all your feedback, comments, clarity of vision, and any new ideas we've had. It's almost like we have to write the book before we know what we're writing about.

"Then, I hand that version to you. You share it with a couple of people who'll give you honest feedback—your spouse and a business partner, for example—and then we'll come back together. You'll say, 'Derek, here's what we need to change.' I'll say, '[Name], after coming back to it with fresh eyes, here's what I think we need to do.'

"I'll go do another round of editing, not only addressing any changes but also making sure that each sentence and paragraph is smooth and tight. At the end of that, I pass it off to two proofreaders in succession, and then, my friend, you'll have a manuscript.

"Now, I can help you weigh the pros and cons of pursuing a traditional publisher or self-publishing, but either way, you'll have an industry-standard manuscript.

"Okay, so now that I've just stood you in front of a fire hydrant of information, let me stop and ask: Any questions on any of that, on my four-step process?"

(Wait for inevitable variation of, "No, that all makes sense.")

"The beauty of this approach is that each step of the way allows you to gain further clarity on your vision for the book. The clearer you are about your vision, the more clearly you can communicate that to me, and the more clearly I can translate that into your book so that your book embodies your vision.

"I'll tell you the highest compliment I ever received as a professional ghostwriter. I worked with a consultant who wouldn't let her husband read any drafts of the manuscript—partly, I think, because she wanted to develop her ideas on her own and partly, I think, just to piss him off. When she finally let him read a nearly finished draft, she printed it out, and he went to read it on the couch. A couple of hours later, she had to walk through the living room on her way to the kitchen and her husband looked up from the manuscript and said, 'Oh my god—this sounds just like you!'

"That is when I knew I'd done my job: when your own husband thinks that your book sounds just like you. That's the highest compliment a professional ghostwriter could ever receive."

(Wait for response.)

Steps 5 and 6: Trial close and Dealing with objections.

(For my sales process, I usually don't uncover an objection—if any—until after presenting my prices and asking what their budget is.)

"Okay, so the big question, of course, is, 'How much does it cost?' Let me walk you through the different packages I offer, starting with the most inclusive and working our way down."

(Describe three service levels—turnkey, core service, and coaching—and flat fee for each, beginning with the most expensive. Yes, Matthew helped me create those, too.)

"So, I realize, of course, that writing a thought leadership book is a marketing investment, and your investment has to justify its cost. What budget did you have in mind for your book?"

(Wait for response.)

(If I detect a hesitation on price): *"Well, I completely understand needing to think about it. It's a big investment of time and money, but let me leave you with one quick story as food for thought.*

"I once had a financial adviser who came to me wanting to write a book that wasn't just about how to manage your money but about how to leave a lasting financial legacy. The book itself was to be his legacy to his child.

"But, being a guy who spent his days managing other people's investments, he just couldn't justify the cost of his book in his mind.

"Two years later, he finally came back and said, 'Derek, I just can't get it out of my head. I've got to write this book.' He wrote the check, we signed the papers, and we finally got started on a book that we'd have been finished with if he had started back when he knew he really needed to write it."

(Otherwise): "I tell you what: Why don't I draw up a draft of what our agreement would look like, send it over, and let you look through it. We can schedule a follow-up call for next week to talk about it. Does that sound good?

"Awesome. Well, look, [name], I've been doing this long enough to know to look for two main things in calls like these. The first is that I make the author laugh. The second is that the author makes me laugh. If two strangers can get on the phone and make each other laugh, that's usually indicative of how the relationship is going to go. And the better we work together, the better the book will be."

(Wait for response.)

"Alright. Well, it was great to meet you and I look forward to exploring this further with you."

Seriously. That's all I do. Six figures a year. Year after year.

WHY BOTHER?

Derek's script may seem long. You may be thinking that it's a lot of work to come up with this and memorize it. But the joke I used to tell my team at the Pollard Institute was that people memorize entire Shakespeare plays to make $20,000 a year. If they memorized my script, they could make $200,000 a year.

To this day, I still use a script. In fact, my script was put to the test after I spoke at the Electrolux VP Summit in Bangkok. The trip back home was thirty hours long, and I finally arrived home late Thursday night...with twelve sales calls booked for the next day. The opportunity to speak had been last-minute, but moving all of those calls would've been a nightmare. So, I sucked it up and went through all twelve calls, jet-lagged like crazy and struggling to focus. I just used my same script verbatim—maybe with a little (or a lot) less vibrancy—and closed just as many clients as I did on any other day.

Do the work. Make a script. Make a mint.

11

mastery

All sales professionals in the top 10 percent use a planned presentation. The low money earners, those in the bottom 80 percent of salespeople, simply say whatever comes out of their mouths when they meet with customers.

—**BRIAN TRACY,** *The Psychology of Selling*

Those who can't sell, teach.

At least, that's how most salespeople view most sales trainers. So when Thomas's boss brought me in to speak to him and the three-man Colliers sales team, it was no surprise that that's exactly what I saw on their faces: no interest in hearing from yet another blowhard who'd turned to training after deciding he couldn't handle the hard-core world of sales anymore.

To be polite, the bulldog on the team asked me how my Thanksgiving had gone the week before.

"Oh, it was good. Just cut short."

Naturally, he asked why it'd been cut short.

I said, "Well, I had to go to bed early Thursday night as I had two TV interviews early the next morning. Of course, the rest of the family stayed up late enjoying themselves and making a racket laughing, so I got no sleep. I had to roll into KXAN at 5:30 and then into the FOX studio at 7:15. Another guest at FOX recognized me from my 5:30 segment and struck up a conversation, and then asked, 'How are you getting all this free media? It cost me a lot of money for the opportunity to get on this show.' I told him I'm just really good at finding the right hook and telling a good story to the news desk.

"Anyway, long story short, he asked me to come in for a whiteboard session at his company yesterday to explain what I was doing. After the session, they were so impressed, they asked me if I'd be interested in speaking at their convention, which is one of the biggest stages in America.

"So, in short, my Thanksgiving got cut into a bit, but all in all, it worked out great."

I paused for a beat because I could tell they were blown away. Then I said, "So, tell me what I just did there."

They looked at each other, lost.

I said, "I could see on your faces when I walked in that you all had objections in your head about getting sales training. I used a true story jam-packed with credibility points to side-step that objection so you could see me and this training for what it could be—and what I'll ensure it will be: amazing. So let's get to it."

One of them told me afterward that when I told that story, all he could think was, *Oh, wow, this guy is the real deal!*

If I hadn't started off with that little story, I don't know that two hard-core salesmen and a motivated introvert would now have "story time" marked in their calendars each week. Even though I'd already booked three training sessions in my meeting with the firm's principals, I had to also sell the value of that training to the salesmen themselves. After all, training people who haven't bought in to what I'm saying in the first place makes it hard to get results—and I am always focused on getting every one of my clients real-world return on their investment.

I could have said, "Your bosses have already paid for this;

you have to be here, so sit down and listen up." But that wouldn't have helped them. I could have just ignored the facial expressions and started training an unreceptive audience and hoped they eventually came around. Instead, I did a spur-of-the-moment sales pitch, won the "sale," and went on to have a great relationship with those guys...and used that exact story for the rest of the week anytime a prospective customer asked me how my Thanksgiving went.

In fact, I got the bulldog to come into Alex Murphy's studio and record a case study for me. In it, he says that he didn't buy into my crap at first, but the results were there—and he wouldn't be in front of that camera if they weren't.

That kind of goes against everything we've just talked about in the book up to this point, doesn't it? From preparation, practice, and "run program" to doing something on the fly and just winging it? Seems incongruent.

In actuality, it's just being really good at the introvert's edge.

Once you get your sales system working, you'll be ready to take on 80 percent of the sales situations that come your way. If you don't read any further than this point and put everything I've presented into practice, you'll still do amazingly well: better than 90 percent of your competitors. Plus, you won't have to hustle nearly as hard! You'll find that telling your core stories becomes natural. Then you'll get good at incorporating new stories. Eventually, you'll get good at incorporating new stories on the fly (like I did for Colliers).

It's like learning to ride a bicycle. At first, you need training wheels; that's what the examples in this book are for. Then, you learn the basics of riding; that's what the seven steps are for.

Once you get really good, you can start doing handstands and wheelies; that's what this chapter is for.

EVERYONE LOVES OPTIONS

The seven steps help you focus on your primary customer type. But what about secondary types? Or what if you sell two quite different services? What if you have two different versions of a product: one for residential and one for commercial? Well, then you'll need more than one offering…as well as the awareness to choose the appropriate one for the situation at hand.

What if you sell one-on-one as well as group training for, say, marketing consulting? The information might be similar but the sale and delivery are quite different. With the first, you're selling to individuals buying coaching and consulting for themselves for a period of time. With the other, you're selling a one-time event to someone buying training on behalf of employees in their company. They'd vary greatly in the deliverable, the amount of direct contact, and the price…and you'd need to be prepared to articulate exactly what the differences are. Obviously, you'd need two different approaches.

We identified one of Derek's challenges as having only one product to sell to one type of client: high-end ghostwriting. Sure, he did some editing here or there, but he muddled through the process to make those sales. By and large, if you couldn't afford his price tag, he didn't know what to do with you.

He knew how to deliver more than just ghostwriting, but he

didn't know how to sell it. Once we got him comfortable with selling, we expanded his inventory of programs so that when he recognized that a prospect couldn't afford ghostwriting, he knew how to sell a coaching arrangement instead. He's approaching six-figures in earnings on non-ghostwriting services from a half-dozen authors in just two years.

If you have only one package, you're putting yourself in a box.

PREPARING TO SCALE

On a factory line, it doesn't matter who operates the machinery: The same raw material goes in and the same uniform product comes out.

It doesn't (or shouldn't) matter who comes in to work that day. It doesn't matter if someone's on vacation or takes a sick day. As long as the operator follows the same process, the same thing happens up and down the assembly line.

Sales works the same way. Or, at least, it can.

For the sales teams I've managed and hired, I don't ask the salespeople to come up with their own approach to selling. I don't need them to be creative. I don't need outgoing people. I just need people who can "run program."

These days, I almost always hire introverts. They don't have any bad habits to undo. They don't plan to rely on their charm and conversational skills because they usually don't believe they have them. (It's not true, of course. They just get so nervous trying to sell that their own personality gets buried beneath their anxiety.) They need a system.

In the advantages column: They are detail-oriented, so they do the paperwork correctly and take great notes during meetings. Those who've managed extroverts know this is often a recurring nightmare. Introverts are great listeners, naturally given to focusing more on what the customer is really saying.

As I mentioned earlier, when a salesperson of mine ran into a sales slump, my very first question was, "Are you sticking to the script?" Nine times out of ten, they weren't. They'd gotten overconfident, they'd summarized parts, they had ad-libbed—something had changed. When they returned to the script, they saw their sales climb back to normal.

"But Matthew," you might be saying, "doesn't that go against what you've said about being sincere and authentic? Wouldn't I be forcing someone to follow a sales system designed for me, not them? Wouldn't I be making them tell *my* jokes and *my* stories?"

First, you've already proved that your process works with the clientele you target and attract. That's the baseline. Second, being able to rely on a proven process allows salespeople to relax and follow the flow (just like you). They can be genuine and sincere because they don't have to worry about their individual performance. Third, they can leverage the stories of the entire organization as opposed to just their own. Effectively, they start with decades of experience instead of little to none.

The three-man team at Colliers didn't use stories of their own to quadruple the number of appointments they made and start locking in the whales; they spoke to the three principals—Volney, Doug, and Marc—who combined had a hundred years of commercial real estate experience. The team approached the founders with their list of the most common objections and then asked for a story of a prospect with the same objection who became a client and had a successful outcome. When they went out to sell, they told the stories not as "I had a client who…" but as "We had a client who…"

But when should your team start experimenting on their own? I wouldn't allow it. If you have a team of just three salespeople (plus yourself), it's nearly impossible to keep track of what works and what doesn't if all three are trying different experiments at the same time. Only the lead salesperson gets to try out new things (ideally, that would always be you). If everybody replaces one story with another and sales go up, then you know that story works.

Just like in a factory line, you don't allow the various operators to redesign the entire system whenever they want to. There's one system, one process: yours.

This may seem like it assumes a basic mistrust of salespeople—and employees in general—but it's really more about quality control. If you're in charge of a sales team, it's ultimately your ass on the line. A salesperson might just go find another job. However, if you're the business owner or manager, you're still responsible for delivering the numbers. You want to create a process that works, regardless of who works it.

I know this flies in the face of sales culture, but you actually don't want to rely on superstars, rock stars, and hotshots. If sales were a factory line, these would be your statistical anomalies. It doesn't matter that those anomalies produce a superior product: The problem is that your sales process isn't reliable. Plus, if one operator can consistently produce superior results, it means that the rest of your operators are running your product line at suboptimal levels. In short, if one person can do it, every person should do it.

If you do have a superstar in your employ, it doesn't mean you should run out and fire that person for not following your process. When I first became a sales manager, I enjoyed the sales that came from these types, and I even learned some of their stories and tricks for myself. I used them to create and perfect my script for the whole team. At that point, I didn't even bother to train the rock star. Soon, the results of the process showed. While the rock star shone bright on some days, the introverts beat that person across the board. Soon the rock star would walk into my office and say, "What is this script you've been teaching everyone else?"

When you introduce scripts to your team, two things will happen. Your superstars will either come into your office wanting to know about "this script thing" or they'll move on to another job. Either way, you're no longer reliant on them. You're diversified and your business is safe.

DON'T SURRENDER YOUR BUSINESS

Most business owners and executives hate sales.

Entrepreneurs start businesses because they have an idea or a skill, not because they know how to sell. Corporate executives move up the corporate ladder because of a skill; the salespeople usually make too much money on their commissions to take a pay cut by moving into a salaried position. When you look at the CEOs of the *Fortune* 500, few started out in sales.

Most had a professional skill (engineering, finance, law) and then worked their way up the ranks to become COO or CFO before taking over the helm.

As such, the people at the top of a business don't want to "do" sales. In a larger company, they leave it up to the sales department to magically produce the money. But I've seen businesses suffer major problems by assigning sales to a person or group outside the decision-maker's circle. In large companies, the executives sit so far removed from the customers that they miss crucial conversations and early indicators that their market is changing. When sales becomes a problem, they're not equipped to deal with it. They hire more salespeople or try to incent the ones they have. (Derek and I discovered that *incentivize* isn't a real word. Who knew? Apparently, not us.) They throw money at the problem, hoping it will solve itself.

It's worse for small companies. One of the very first people a founder hires is often a salesperson. The founders want to quickly get out of selling so they can focus on what they're good at. They let the sales guy (or gal) go out and drum up business while they stay at their desk or workbench doing the actual work.

Don't even think about doing this!

When you do, you hand control of your company and your well-being over to someone you just met. If they know how to bring in the money, they can hold you hostage. They can demand larger commissions in exchange for continuing to provide your sole source of revenue and customers. Also, in this model, you become the bottleneck. The salesperson can sell only as much as you have the capacity to deliver.

If you have a sales system, it's easier to hire technicians to do the work and train them to do it as well as you. If you learn how to hire and train for technical skill, then you can continually add on more capacity as you're able to sell it. You can hire salespeople, too. The sky's the limit.

I'm not telling you to be the primary salesperson for the life of your business. I'm just telling you that you can't hand sales off to someone else until you've mastered the process. If your salesperson walks out on you, you can step in until you replace them.

WHEN SALES AND MARKETING WORK IN UNISON

In a testimonial video he did for me, Derek said that he's still not great at sales. He says he's just "decent" (though I think he doesn't give himself enough credit).

"But we put decent marketing with decent sales and...well, I have doubled what I charge my clients," he says in the video.

Even if you already have a good marketing system in place, like he did, it can improve when you start leveraging what you learn from your success in sales. Take me, for instance: I didn't realize that so many of the people I consulted for had introverted personalities until I started looking at who experienced the biggest results from working with me. Once I realized they saw themselves as introverts, I started marketing rapid growth to introverts. I didn't set out to help introverts, but now that I know that's who my marketing attracts, I can be more intentional in speaking directly to them.

Once you find a story that works well, it makes sense to go ahead and use it in your marketing, doesn't it? In your ads, your website copy, your social media, your direct mailings, and anywhere else people might find you.

Depending on the medium, it may not pack the same punch as you telling it in person, but it's better than generic two-for-one coupons or the same promise of "safe, fast, and reliable."

In fact, the better you know your customers, the better you can speak directly to them and their situation. In his sales calls, Derek heard over and over again that the person would sit down at the computer, pull up Microsoft Word, write "Chapter One" at the top of the page, get ready to start writing the book...and freeze. "It's like all my years of experience suddenly fly out the window. My mind's as blank as the screen," one guy told him. Once he heard this a number of times, what did Derek do? He started using that story all over his website and online ads.

One objection Alex Murphy heard over and over was that the business had "done a video and it didn't do anything for us." Once he and I discussed this—and he explained to me why a single video in isolation doesn't work—I rebranded him as "the narrative strategist."

Today, when people ask what that is, he gets to explain why a video or even a standalone video campaign doesn't work. Your video marketing has to have a narrative arc across time and media. It's the art of crafting a strong story across the videos, all sharing that same narrative. Suddenly, prospects understand that Alex is much more than just another video guy.

So I've given you a bunch of quick examples about how

strong marketing can support strong sales. However, to dive deeper into the topic, the best way for me to explain it is to share the exact scripted story I use with all of my prospects.

Let me give you an example.

Wendy was a client of mine who taught Mandarin to kids and adults in California. One of the problems that she had was that she was struggling to charge $50 to $80 an hour for private language tuition. This was because there were so many other language coaches moving from other states into California willing to cut their prices to the bone, charging just $30 to $50 an hour to get their first client success stories. Wendy paid her staff more than that.

Also, because we now live in a global economy, she also had to deal with people from China offering their services for $10 to $15 an hour on Craigslist. She was losing current clients and was struggling to get new clients.

She asked me, "How do I compete in this crowded market where all I have to compete on...is price?"

I said, "Wendy, competing on price is a long road to the bottom, where the only person who wins actually loses, because they have to provide the service for well below what they are worth. I'd prefer to help you avoid the battle altogether."

After reviewing the hundreds and hundreds of clients Wendy had worked with, there were two customers—just two—that she helped with so much more than just language tutoring.

The first thing she helped them with was understanding the concept of guanxi. *The first time I heard it I thought they meant galaxy and they were talking about outer space, but this is actually the Chinese word for rapport.*

See, if you and I had a sales meeting here in the United States or back home in Australia, at the end of that meeting I would ask you (if I was horrible at sales) if you would like to buy my product or service. If you said you wanted to think about it, I'd call you back the following week. If you still said you wanted to think about it, well, we know my chances of making that sale are going down and down, right?

(Small pause to let customer respond.)

Well, in China they will want to go out to dinner four or five times before they even want to talk business. They will probably even want to see you drunk over karaoke once or twice.

(Wait for small chuckle.)

But here is why: They are generally not talking about transactional, twelve- or fourteen-month deals like we do in the West. They are talking about fifty- to one-hundred-year contracts.

I mean this is longer than a lot of people's marriages and lifetimes. So, for them, it's more important to know the person they are getting into bed with than the specific terms of a contract.

The second thing she helped them with was understand-

ing the difference between e-commerce in China and e-commerce in the Western world.

The third was the importance of respect. Wendy helped her clients understand that, while it's great to learn Mandarin, if they don't at least try to reduce their accent it's seen as disrespectful and then they're not doing business in China. Now, they don't expect you to sound exactly like them, but they do expect you to at least try.

It's the same as when someone hands you a business card in China. In the Western world, when we get a card at a networking event, we don't even look at the card. We just throw it in our pocket and keep on chatting. Then we get home and pull these cards out of our pocket and we are like, "Who is that again?" Well, in China, you are expected to hold the card, cherish it, look at it, turn it over, appreciate the back, then finally pull out your card case, almost bow, put the card in your card case, and then keep on talking. Again, anything less than that, it's disrespectful.

I mean, I just got back from speaking at Electrolux in Bangkok and saw this firsthand. Over one hundred vice presidents in the room and each time I handed one of them my card—a person who is responsible for hundreds if not thousands of staff—they would take my card and do exactly that.

So Wendy was helping these executives with these three things, and I said, "Wendy, you're doing so much more for these people than just private language tutoring. Tell me, what are you doing for these people?"

She said, "What do you mean? These are just little things. I'm just trying to help."

I said, "No. Wendy, you're stuck in your functional skill. Is it fair to assume that, as a result of working with these clients, they're going to be more successful in China?"

She replied, "Well, yeah, I hope so."

I said, "Great, so why don't we call you the 'China Success Coach,' and why don't we call your product the 'China Success Intensive'?"

This would be a five-week program that worked with the executive, the spouse, and any children being relocated across to China.

The program didn't teach Mandarin; after all, Mandarin education was seen as a commodity (and Wendy agreed it was better to let the other companies fight that one out). It focused on just the core elements that she taught executives being relocated to China.

Now, you're probably wondering, why the spouse and children? Well, we're all in business and, of course, selling to more people means you can charge more money. But secondly, think about it: If you're an executive being relocated to China and you get there and your spouse or child is not happy, well then, you're probably going to get constantly called home to deal with an unhappy family, greatly reducing the chances of the executive succeeding. It's so vitally important that the whole family unit be successful when they get there.

Wendy, excited by the idea, then asked me, "So would I reach out to sell this to executives?"

I said, "Actually no. Think about it: Who is your customer?"

She said, "Oh, you're right…it would be the companies."

I said, "No, your ideal customer is going somewhere already, and it's easier to work with the third party they're already working with: immigration attorneys. See, when I first moved to the United States, I needed to get a visa and then, after that, a green card. Every time, I went through an immigration attorney."

I said, "They have relationships with all the people you are hoping to work with. They are your ideal clients."

So, we went to some of these immigration attorneys who charge between $2,000 and $5,000 to get a client, organize all of the paperwork required to get a visa approved, and then deal with all of the bureaucracy to ensure that it happens. And we said to them, "How would you like to make a $3,000 commission for any successful introduction to an executive being relocated to China?"

They said, "That's more than what we generally make after costs for doing the visa! What would I have to say?"

We said, "Just say this: 'Congratulations. You've now been approved to go and work in China. Now, I just want to double-check: Are you as ready as you could be to be relocated across to China?' When they say, 'Yeah. We've got our visa thanks to you; we have learned Mandarin. In fact, the kids are getting pretty good at it, too, and we've got our house organized. I'd say we're good'—whatever their answer, you respond with, 'No, there is a lot more to it than that. I think you need to speak to the China Success Coach.' That's it."

Wendy would then get on a call with the easiest sale in the world. I mean, these executives were terrified. I just moved from Australia to the United States and I was terrified. Imagine being relocated to a place that doesn't even speak the same language.

The companies were also terrified. They generally had millions if not billions of dollars riding on the success or failure of these executives, so they wanted to do everything possible to ensure the success of the executives when they got there.

So, Wendy charged $30,000 for this five-week program and after paying a $3,000 commission to the immigration attorney, she made $27,000 for the easiest sale in the world instead of struggling every single day to fight for $50 to $80 an hour. That's the power of a strong and unified message.

For you, you have to look at what your unique differentiators are. Everyone has unique experiences, a unique upbringing, unique past customers, and a unique education that perfectly qualifies them to provide a unique and highly valuable service to one specific group of people.

Once you discover who those customers are, the unified message is easy.

For Wendy, it was guanxi, e-commerce, and respect, the higher-level benefit being China success.

For me, I'm a business coach, a branding expert, a sales strategist, a social media specialist; I'm a master in neurolinguistic programming; I'm so many things and nobody cares. But when I say I'm the rapid growth guy, that I help organizations large and small obtain rapid growth, the power of that message gets me heard in a crowded market.

That's what happens when sales and marketing work together.

THE INTROVERT'S EDGE

So now you understand the process of selling...but what exactly is the introvert's edge?

You may have guessed it was your compassion, your empathy, your understanding, your unique ability to listen intently, or perhaps your ability to thoroughly prepare. But the benefits these traits offer are no secret. Plenty of research and literature underscores the advantages of these natural qualities of introverts.

The introvert's edge is knowing how to utilize your natural strengths in a systematic and focused way. Those skills are the raw elements; this book, the catalyst; the transformation, sales illiteracy to sales mastery.

Armed with the techniques, strategies, and process within these pages, you now have the edge you've been looking for to go out and outsell anyone.

As Admiral David Farragut once said—and as my father often repeated—"Damn the torpedoes, full speed ahead!"

ABOUT THE AUTHOR

In primary school, I told a teacher that I wanted to be a lawyer. My teacher told me to "set more realistic expectations."

I grew up in Craigieburn, Australia. People from my town don't run businesses (or if they do, they're blue-collar). People who want to do any better than how they were born suffer what we call in Australia "tall poppy syndrome": the tallest flower in the field gets cut down. It's best not to be seen as trying too hard or dreaming too big.

After I got promoted to a sales manager, my company moved me to Adelaide. When I came home one weekend for a party, I met up with an old classmate who had been one of the "cool kids" in school. When catching up, he related that he'd found a job at a local factory.

"Matt," he said, "you did it right. You were one of the smart ones. Growing up, I'd always believed that I should focus on enjoying my life in the moment, not worrying too much about the future. Now, I spend all day working in front of a furnace. It's hot as hell. I wish I'd worked as hard as you did to get out and make something of myself."

This was news to me. I'd always felt stupid as the try-hard kid. The reason I spent hour upon hour in school was because

I was always so far behind everyone else. My Irlen Syndrome wasn't diagnosed until I was seventeen years old. I graduated with the reading speed of a sixth-grader.

But maybe that was a blessing in disguise. Maybe if I'd had the same natural abilities as my classmate then, I would have been part of the status quo. Maybe my disability pushed me to become something more than I would have been otherwise. I like to say that our failures seed the success of our future.

I think it works the same way for introverts because we don't have the same natural abilities as extroverts. We have to make up for it in other ways...but that extra effort actually gives us an edge over others.

The rules of the game never seemed to work for me. I've always had to create my own by necessity. For instance, just eighteen months into launching my first company, I was in a pool hall with friends when a guy on the other side of the room, strung out on meth, went crazy. He broke a glass bottle and attacked me, tearing a gash across my face; he missed blinding me by mere millimeters. It took twenty-six stitches, painful plastic surgery, and a total of five years to heal. I had just begun to build my self-confidence, but a disfiguring scar killed all that.

Before, I looked like an innocent, acne-riddled, nerdy high school kid who couldn't tell a lie if he tried. With the scar, I looked like a biker just come from a bar fight. Even a year later, the scar still looked raw, especially because the doctors had to keep reopening it as part of my recovery.

My appearance no longer established trust naturally. I had to redesign my sales process to actually overcome people's instinctive *mistrust* of me (leading to the credibility step that later became integral to my system).

Somehow, it worked.

I was making more money than I'd ever dreamed of. I had the nicest car, the best clothes, and lived in an embarrassingly expensive penthouse overlooking Melbourne. During the city's annual business awards program, I found myself up on stage receiving the prestigious Young Achiever Award. Not only was I successful, but everyone else saw me as a success, too. I had it all. I was living the dream.

I vividly remember the feeling after coming home to my penthouse and putting my award on the shelf: miserable disillusion. I decided I needed to do more. Over the next several years, I launched more businesses, earned more money, transformed whole markets, and reached even more success. But nothing was enough; nothing filled that enormous gap in my soul.

I decided to take a break and travel the world for a year, hoping I'd discover . . . something. I partied at Carnival in Brazil and Coachella in California. I went shipwreck diving off Gibraltar and meandered through the Swiss Alps. I stood atop Iguazu Falls. I hiked to the overlook of Machu Picchu. I even ran with the bulls in Spain.

I was searching my soul, even as I was searching the world... and I discovered something.

All the "success" I'd chased wasn't really about getting those things. I didn't actually care about the car, the penthouse, or the notoriety. I discovered that I'd pursued all those things because I wanted to prove to the world that I wasn't some little learning-disabled kid worth nothing. Well, I'd proved it. But I still felt empty.

Looking back over my experiences, I remembered when I'd felt the most fulfilled. Out of all my experiences, the Pollard Institute made me the happiest. Helping skilled professionals find confidence to proudly articulate what they do in a way that led to a client who paid them what they were truly worth—and seeing them create a system that enabled that to happen again and again—made such a transformative change in these business heroes' lives. To hear Derek Lewis, Alex Murphy, and others testify about what my advice has done for them still gives me goosebumps.

That's my mission: to bridge the chasm between someone's struggling dream and a rapid growth business they love.

—*Matthew Pollard*

REFERENCES AND FURTHER READING

Aaker, Jennifer. "Harnessing the Power of Stories." Stanford University, Center for the Advancement of Women's Leadership. Accessed May 19, 2017. https://womensleadership.stanford.edu/stories.

Arnsten, Amy, Carolyn M. Mazure, and Rajita Sinha. "Everyday Stress Can Shut Down the Brain's Chief Command Center." *Scientific American*, April 2012.

Cain, Susan. *Quiet: The Power of Introverts in a World That Can't Stop Talking*. London: Penguin Books, 2013.

Cialdini, Robert B. *Influence: The Psychology of Persuasion*. New York: Collins, 2007.

Cialdini, Robert. *Pre-suasion: A Revolutionary Way to Influence and Persuade*. New York: Simon & Schuster, 2016.

Davis, Robert C. *Shipbuilders of the Venetian Arsenal: Workers and Workplace in the Preindustrial City*. Baltimore: Johns Hopkins University Press, 2007.

Deloitte United States. "Navigating the New Digital Divide." November 7, 2016. Accessed May 19, 2017. https://www2.deloitte.com/us/en/pages/consumer-business/articles/navigating-the-new-digital-divide-retail.html.

Gallo, Carmine. *The Storyteller's Secret: From TED Speakers to Business Legends, Why Some Ideas Catch On and Others Don't*. New York: St. Martin's Press, 2016.

Glenn, Joshua, Rob Walker, Eric Reynolds, Jacob Covey, Kristy Valenti, and Michael Wysong. *Significant Objects: 100 Extraordinary Stories About Ordinary Things*. Seattle, WA: Fantagraphics Books, 2012.

Hasson, Uri, Asif A. Ghazanfar, Bruno Galantucci, Simon Garrod, and Christian Keysers. "Brain-to-Brain Coupling: A Mechanism for Creating and Sharing a Social World." *Trends in Cognitive Sciences* 16, no. 2 (2012): 114–121. doi:10.1016/j.tics.2011.12.007.

references and further reading

Loo, Robert. "Note on the Relationship Between Trait Anxiety and the Eysenck Personality Questionnaire." *Journal of Clinical Psychology* 35, no. 1 (1979): 110.

Mar, Raymond A. "The Neural Bases of Social Cognition and Story Comprehension." *Annual Review of Psychology* 62, no. 1 (2011): 103–134. doi:10.1146/annurev-psych-120709-145406.

Schwartz, Barry. *The Paradox of Choice: Why More Is Less.* New York: Harper Collins, 2004.

Shapiro, Kenneth J., and Irving E. Alexander. "Extraversion-Introversion, Affiliation, and Anxiety." *Journal of Personality* 37, no. 3 (1969): 387–406.

Sword, Lesley. "The Gifted Introvert." Gifted and Creative Services Australia, 2000. Accessed May 19, 2017. http://www.giftedservices.com.au.

Zak, Paul J. *Trust Factor: The Science of Creating High-Performance Companies.* New York: AMACOM, 2017.

INDEX

Aaker, Jennifer, 110
ABN, 31
advisors, 69, 125–126
advocates, 93–94
agenda, 27–28, 58–63
  for controlling sales process, 62–63
  in ghostwriting case study, 178–180
  hidden, 58–61
  price discussion in, 143–144
aggressive salespeople, 117–119, 125–
  126
anxiety, 38, 39
ANZ Bank, 43
Apple, 95
asking for sales, 30
asking questions, 28, 67–84, 174
  in double-bind trial close, 133–134
  establishing rapport by, 49–51
  finding solutions by, 68–72
  in ghostwriting case example, 180
  identifying problems by, 82–84
  and listening, 72–75
  in patterns, 72–75
  in series, 78–82
  setting agenda for, 59–60
assembly line, 157
assuming sales, 31–32, 139–153
  closing in first meeting by, 146–151
  overcoming excuses by, 151–153
  and questions about price, 143–146
assumptions, 139–141
Austin, City of, 140
authenticity, 46, 196

Baby Cheetah Plays Piano (Hurley), 102
Baker, Meshell, 132–134
benefits of products, 105, 109–110
Black Mastercard, 96

Botsman, Rachel, 39
Branson, Richard, 95
Buffett, Warren, on testing conditions,
  127
The Business Book Bible (Lewis), 176, 179
business ghostwriting case example,
  167–187
  and benefit of using scripts, 186–187
  current sales process in, 175–177
  former sales process in, 167–173
  marketing in, 200–201
  sales training in, 173–175
  scripts in, 178–186
  secondary customers in, 194–195
but, use of word, 119

Capital One, 140, 152
Carnegie, Dale, on personal connections,
  27
Castrol, 158
Cathcart, Jim, on diagnosing customer
  problems, 65
change(s), 148–149, 162–163
Cialdini, Robert, 46–47, 135
closing, 146–151, *see also* trial close
Colliers International, 117, 119, 121,
  191–193, 196–197
Comer, Jim, 54–56, 80–81, 125
compounding effect, 144
conference call, sales meetings via,
  176–177
confrontation, 28–29
control
  and responsibility for sales, 198–200
  of sales process, 24, 62–63
costs, of customers' problems, 82–84
credibility, 48, 53–58, 192

ACKNOWLEDGMENTS

Derek, for being my biggest cheerleader, for helping me get this process out of my head, for being one of my closest and most trusted conspirators and friends, and for being the amazing soul that you are.

Dad, for pushing me to be better, for always playing devil's advocate, for challenging me to test my perceptions of the world, for giving me the kick in the ass to go into business for myself, and for telling me to damn the torpedoes.

Mum, for being my emotional support, for always being on my side, for not taking no for an answer until you found the solution to my disability that changed my life, and for fostering the heart inside me.

Chelsea, for being the sister everyone wishes they had, for being with me every step of the way, for being my confidante, and for putting up with me all these years.

Gran, for providing us the family time every Thursday night to talk business and for always saying how proud of me you were.

acknowledgments

Brittany, for making me a better man in every way, for being my best friend, and for showing me endless patience and love.

Cindy, for seeing what no one else saw, for challenging me to do it right, and for being the literary agent every author hopes to find.

Tim, for believing this book had a home at AMACOM, for seeing its potential before it even existed, for trusting in my ability to see it through, and for a collaborative spirit that made the book far more than what it would have been.

My clients and sales teams, for letting me use your stories and for allowing me to learn and develop myself through the opportunity of working with you.

My readers, for trusting me to take you on this journey.

—*Matthew Pollard*

BONUS: YOUR EXCLUSIVE INVITATION

THE INTROVERT'S EDGE INNER CIRCLE

If you do everything I've shown you in this book, you'll see a dramatic improvement.

But why stop there?

Join me and other professionals committed to sales success in *The Introvert's Edge* Inner Circle—an online community for introverts just like us.

Not only will you receive instant access to a wealth of additional tools, resources, and exclusive content, but you'll also get direct access to me!

Plenty of books give you bonus material, but have you ever heard of a book that gives you access to the author himself? Well, *The Introvert's Edge* does!

As a thank-you for buying a copy of the book, you get a year's subscription to the Inner Circle—**absolutely free!**

What does the Inner Circle offer? You can:

> Get access to me through live-streams and recorded Q&A sessions

- ▶ Get feedback, support, and encouragement from other introverted entrepreneurs, service providers, and sales professionals just like you
- ▶ Learn how your peers have used the 7 steps to sky-rocket their sales
- ▶ Enjoy hours of video interviews from the people you've already met in the book: Meshell Baker, Derek Lewis, Alex Murphy, Amy Looper, and others
- ▶ Read the Inner Circle-only bonus chapter: something you can relate to if anyone's ever tried to make you feel guilty for trying to succeed
- ▶ Access how-to videos just for *The Introvert's Edge* readers
- ▶ And much, much more. . .

All of this for an *entire year*—just to say thank you for reading! See you in the Inner Circle!

www.theintrovertsedge.com/innercircle

—Matthew Pollard

Printed in the USA
CPSIA information can be obtained
at www.ICGtesting.com
JSHW030400290524
63614JS00018B/213

9 780814 438879